NOW THAT YOU ARE MARRIED

By
ALEXANDER GYIMAH AGYEMANG
Relationship Series

DEDICATION

To my wife for over twelve years and my sweetheart for over eighteen years, Mrs. Irene Gyimah Agyemang

COPYRIGHT PAGE

Now That You Are Married

© **Alexander Gyimah Agyemang**

First Published in July, 2023

Unless otherwise stated all scripture quotations are from the New International Version of the Bible © 2011 and the King James Version of the Bible© 1987.

ISBN:9798853144873

All rights reserved. No part of this publication may be reproduced, stored in a retrieval system, or transmitted in any form or by any means-electronic, mechanical, photocopying, recording or otherwise without prior permission from the author.

ENLIGHTENED WORD TEACHING MINISTRY

C/O Post, Office Box 783, Takoradi Western Region, Ghana / West Africa

E-mail: lexgyi@yahoo.com or lexgyi@gmail.com

Lexgyi.blogspot.com

Instagram: lexgyi

Facebook.com / lexgyi@yahoo.com

Youtube: Alexander Gyimah Agyemang

Twitter.com/LEXGYI

OTHERS BOOKS BY AUTHOR

1) Fear versus Faith: The Battle for the Control of Your Destiny

2) 15 Things I Wish I Had Mastered By Age 30 For Maximum Achievement

3) 5 Things I Wish I Had Mastered By Age 30 For A Life Of Excellence

4) 20 Things I Wish I Had Mastered By Age 30 For A Life Of Excellence

5) But :Keys for Turning Sinking Sand Into Stepping Stones

6) His Great Grace Breaks Barriers

7) Temptations Trials and Tests

8) Going Back To Eden: Recreating The Best Environment For Fruitfulness and Multiplication

9) Familiarity and The Anointing

10) Friends: Allies, Competitors Or Enemies

11) Surviving The Worst Pandemic In Human History: Is God Responsible For Covid-19

FOREWORD

Usually the expectations of every single person before marriage is mostly high, for this reason when these expectations are somehow not met the person becomes disappointed because he or she thought that 'I know him or her very well'. This is where they start singing the song of 'he has changed or she has changed'. In this book, our author has insightfully and prayerfully put together this wonderful piece to educate couples that: it is not possible to know all about your spouse before you getting married. This is actually hard truth to most new couples.

There are some hidden attitudes that one would never show even in years of dating but will show up in marriage. It is therefore expedient for couples to understand that we are married to imperfect beings and through our marriage we have a responsibility to try to make ourselves better people. The average human being cannot have it all, there are always shocks in marriage when you get to discover that your spouse has some imperfections in their bodies, knowledge and even speech. Some husbands these days only discover the real shape of their wives after marrying them because they are used to wearing artificial hips etc. Others also discover that their spouses are addicted to certain "bad" habits and this becomes a problem that one has to deal with or manage for the rest of their lives.

We therefore need to understand that these surprising traits will not disappear in a twinkle of an eye, but it will take time for your partner to adjust. Because people take time to grow these habit, spouse need to have patience in their expectation of them to reform. Instead of calling them names because the reform is taking longer than expected. Change is always gradual. There are some wives or husbands who have very weird ideologies which can harm the trust between them and their spouses. These are things that have to be dealt with seriously or managed wisely, as it has the tendency to destroy the marriage.

The author, has made it clear that these are not normal. Example, I know of a Christian wife who has now removed her rings and earrings and has also stopped taking care of her hair because of these misguided ideologies. But such changes when discovered in good time and the couple spoken to by someone they respect, they can be persuaded from them. Additionally we advices that couples discuss or seek help where necessary.

In our world today, where knowledge is abounding with many misleading theologies and ideologies, I believe this is a must read book for every couple and upcoming young ones. The bible declares in the book of John 8:32 - "Then you will know the truth and the truth will set you free". As you read this book may your spirit man be enlighten and may you know the purpose of God for you, Now that you are married.

Ps Samuel and Mrs Perdita Asiamah

PIWC Kwadaso Resident Minister

June 2023

TABLE OF CONTENTS

CONTENTS	PAGE
Dedication…………………………………………	ii
Copyright…………………………………………	iii
Other Books By Author…………………………	iv
Foreword …………………………………………	v
Table of Contents………………………………	vii
Chapter 1 - You Will Notice Your Spouse Is Not Perfect………………………	1
Chapter 2 - You Will Need To Learn To Do Things For Reasons Other Than Your Feelings. ……………………	7
Chapter 3 - You Will Notice Your Spouse Has Addictions You Did Not Know They Had During Courtship………………………	12
Chapter 4 - You Will Notice Your Spouse Knows People You Were Not Aware Of During Courtship …………………	18
Chapter 5 - You Will Notice That There Are Some Things In Your Spouses Past You Were Not Aware Of………………………………	23
Chapter 6 - You Will Suddenly Become Aware	

Of Weaknesses You Did Not Know
You Have.. 29

Chapter 7 - You Will Become Aware Of Strengths
You Did Not Know You Have..................... 35

Chapter 8 - You Will Deal With Issues You Never
Had Before In Your Life............................. 40

Chapter 9 - You Will Need To Make Room In Your
Heart And Mind To Accommodate Your
Spouse.. 45

Chapter 10 - You Will Notice That There Will Be
Things You Will Complain About But Your
Spouse Will Be Unable To Stop.................. 50

Chapter 11 - You Will Have Opportunities You Never
Had Before 56

Chapter 12 - Your Togetherness Will Increase
Your Ability To Deal With Some Things................. 62

Chapter 13 - You Will Notice That Your Being
Married Will Make Dealing With Some
Situations Harder. 66

Chapter 14- You Will Need To Modify Your

Outlook Towards Life To Have A
Successful Marriage.................................. 71

Chapter 15- Your Marriage Can Take You To
Places You Never Planned To Go............... 77

Chapter 16- You Will Say No To Things You Never
Thought You Could................................... 83

Chapter 17- You Will Say Yes To Things You
Never Thought You Could......................... 87

Chapter 18- You Will Learn To Change Your
Views On Many Things In Your Life............ 92

Chapter 19 - Your Motivation For Doing Things
Will Mostly Be Members Of Your Family
Instead Of Your Personal Needs............... 98

Chapter 20- You Will Become Aware Of
The Overwhelming Need To Pray
About Your Family................................. 102

Decision Page.. 109

ACKNOWLEDGEMENTS

I will like to thank all the young couples of the Forestry Commission Kumasi who helped to review the book and for their great reviews. I will like to thank especially Mrs.Angela Agyei Darko for editing the whole book and suggesting ways to improve the write up.

CHAPTER 1

YOU WILL NOTICE YOUR SPOUSE IS NOT PERFECT

No One Is Perfect

Psalm 139:14 King James Version

14 I will praise thee; for I am fearfully and wonderfully made: marvellous are thy works; and that my soul knoweth right well.

Even though the above statement is wholly true it does not mean we are flawless or have no buts with our character or nature. So the above scripture is true but it is also true that all human beings have fallen below our good nature. The nature we had when we were first created in the likeness of Elohim. But young love does not make it appear that way. If truly we believe no one is perfect, then why do we call our fiancées or beloveds 'angel'? If we truly believe they have the same tendencies as us, why do men often call them 'princess' or 'queen' to mention a few?

Scientists say, the hormones which are secreted during the time we fall in love make us more adventurous and therefore more forgiving of the one we love. Hence the few recollections of wrongs done. Creating the impression that none has been done. I remember, my own case when I could not call my fiancée then anything but sweet, sweetheart, princess and love. It was exactly how I felt because I believed I was with someone who was the closest to a perfect person on earth.

It is a feeling people have even when they are dating cultists or even armed robbers. Because the evil they hear about their partners might not be happening in that relationship but outside of it. Others believe they are the antidote to whatever bad behaviour the lover is reputed to have. Still others also believe their badly behaved partner's love for them is so strong they will not do them wrong, ever. Hence reinforcing that bubble which says 'he or she loves me too much to misbehave'. Others feel that their partner is not as bad as it is being alleged but it is because he or she has not been understood and hence their actions misinterpreted by the society or acquaintances to be unreasonable or bad.

But I am not even talking about these extreme situations where cultist or robbers have changed behaviours because they fell in love with a God fearing woman. No! I am talking about the fact that our hearts and minds exaggerate how good our spouses to be are, so we can feel comfortable deciding to settle down with them for the rest of our lives. In other words, you felt your wife was an angel because you believed you needed an angel to stay with before you can be happy. But what you do not understand is that, you do not need to stay with a perfect person to be happy. Do we even know who a perfect person is?

The Bible says that for a good person somebody may die for him or her if necessary but for a perfect person no one would. Have we asked ourselves why perfect people are not liked? Because their actions and sayings will constantly remind you that you are not perfect. Again a perfect person may be too perfect for an imperfect being like you, who has only interacted with imperfect people throughout your life.

Thus living with a perfect partner may turn out to be the opposite of what you expected it to be. Because what you need is an agreeable person and not someone who never does anything wrong. Most of us want perfect people though we know we are not perfect ourselves because we think perfection is the same as accommodation. Because in our selfishness we want their perfection to make up for our imperfections. We desire to be with a perfect person because we believe such people will accommodate our excesses whilst remaining good to us.

In other words, we want a person who will acts as a 'stabilizer' in the marriage or relationship, absorbing the pains of our foolish acts whilst never passing unto us the pains we might be inflicting upon them on a daily basis. But after marriage you will realise that, as a couple our bad behaviour if not forgiven may influence our partner to return the 'favour' in one form or another. Then it becomes a race to the bottom, as to who can show the other that they 'can really go bad.'

You Will Notice The Imperfections of Your Spouse In The following Areas

Imperfections In body

You will realise that not every part of your partner is the way you thought it will be. Suddenly you will realise that their ears are too big or small. You may suddenly notice or realise they do not have as much hair as you thought they did. And more interestingly you may notice they do not smell good all the time, as you have become accustomed to anytime you went out on a date. Especially after a long sleep when they open their mouth to speak. But you know this yourself! Since you yourself experience this every morning before you brush your teeth. Do not take the efforts that your spouse has made to look and smell good to you for all the years you were dating or courting for granted at all. It was done to impress you.

Imperfections In Knowledge

You may be shocked to hear your spouse complaining that: you snore. And may sometimes think it is a make or break thing for the marriage going forward. Something so serious they wonder how they are going to sleep for the rest of the marriage! Only for them to put on weight later and snore even louder than you! Later in the marriage you will notice things which do not bother you, offend your partner greatly because if his or her understanding of life or relationships. You will notice your spouse lacks knowledge in things you thought he or she was perfect in and wonder how you missed it. You will noticed that the social etiquettes and lessons you picked from years of watching movies, she might not have because she was not allowed to watch movies as a child. You might expect her to respond to you in certain ways but he or she might be clueless concerning your expectations because they may never have had that exposure. And yes all these may come up despite six years of a sexual or even non sexual pre marriage relationship.

An example may be: A husband who thinks because the wife can cook, she should be able to cook any food at all. And a wife who may think her husband should be able to fix electrical things in the house because daddy used to fix them but he may not be able to. This should not be a reason to think he is less of a man but to understand that he may be a man with a different set of skills.

Imperfections In Behaviour

Remember, you do not know someone well enough as a husband or wife till they actually become a husband or a wife. No other relationship no matter its similar characteristics prepares people enough to know all about their spouses before they actually marry them. If this situation was not the case, then marriage sustainability should be increasing in the western world where most couples stay together for long periods before they marry. However, marriages are instead ending up in even more divorces despite the couple sometimes having stayed or even parented children together before the marriage.

These changes occur because the marriage accords the couple more rights and privileges which in turn leads to people being less cautious about how they treat each other. You will realise that just as you have bad habits that you have tried to hide during the relationship, your spouse also has bad habits too he or she is busy hiding. So before it hits you in the face, understand that your spouse has some bad habits that you did not notice before marriage. An example of this might be: You may notice your spouse talking in his or her sleep or even sleep walking sometimes. You should not look down on him or her because of it but rather know they may not even be aware of it until you draw their attention to it.

Imperfections That Come From Innocence and Naivety

You may wonder, dear reader why I have included this in the list of things which produces imperfection in the lovely spouse you just married you? Do not get me wrong, innocence gives room for you as a couple to mould each other into the form you desire. However there are spouses who are not only innocent but also naïve. In other words, they just did not avoid doing the wrong things growing up but are also not aware of how to do the right things their partner desire. In other ward, you may not just marry a virgin but someone who also has the habit of thinking sex makes her less spiritual.

You may marry a virgin who never initiates sex nor participate during sex because she thinks it will make her look immoral before her husband. There are marriages which have broken down, though the wife was a virgin before she married because she never appreciated anything her husband did for her. She was obsessed with the fact that she had kept herself for her husband and therefore expected him to do things for her which were frankly unreasonable. Nothing he did was good enough for this perfect wife who believed he was lucky to marry her.

There are other perfect wives who have no idea how other women go the extra mile to keep their husbands. Such women who due to their past exemplary life in the church never had difficulties receiving proposals from suitors take marriage for granted. Such wives often think of the many good brothers they had to reject to marry you, the current husband.

Being innocent and naïve, they never think of the many good ladies their husbands also overlooked to choose them.

The same is true for men who had never been with a carnal woman and therefore underestimate the importance of having a God fearing women in their houses. God fearing men who rate the colour or beauty of a woman over her genuine love for God have also had the shock of their lives concerning the attitude of their trophy wives to spiritual activities they once considered routine. Innocence should not translate into ignorance under any circumstances.

There is a very good reason why the Bible teaches men to live with their wives according to knowledge. I had a mantra growing up because of some of these imperfections of innocence I encountered with spiritual brethren: I am innocent but not naïve. And I believe this mantra should be on the lips of every victorious Christian before and after marriage. The fact that you do not do evil things does not mean you should not appreciate the value of those who do good things.

PRAYER NUGGETS

YOU WILL NOTICE YOUR SPOUSE IS NOT PERFECT

1) You will notice the imperfections of your spouse in the following areas: body, knowledge and behaviour.
1) You will notice imperfections which result purely because of naivety or innocence.
2) You will notice imperfections you did not notice earlier because you were so consumed with the passion of young love.

CHAPTER 2

YOU WILL NEED TO LEARN TO DO THINGS FOR REASONS OTHER THAN YOUR FEELINGS.

You Start With Strong Feelings

Luke 1:26-28 21st Century King James Version

²⁶ And in the sixth month the angel Gabriel was sent from God unto a city of Galilee, named Nazareth, ²⁷ to a virgin espoused to a man whose name was Joseph, of the house of David; and the virgin's name was Mary.

Before humans evolved to the 'I want my way generation' we have today, almost every culture had a system where the adults decided for the young generation who they should marry. This system by and large still exist in the royal families of Europe and Asia to this very day. A king of England once had to abdicate the throne so he could follow his heart to marry an American widow. In 2021, the daughter of the Emperor of Japan after years of insisting she was in love with a commoner eventually lost her princess status so she could marry him. It was a strange sight-seeing this young woman who was once assisted by many aides now going to the supermarket to shop by herself as a commoner.

People have followed their hearts and made tremendous sacrifices along the way to be able to marry the one they love. It is only true feelings that will make Emmanuel Macron, the French president as at 2022, marry a woman who is far older than him. Indeed it is said that initially the wife's daughter thought she was the one he was coming after when he started visiting their house. Only for her to realise later on that it was rather her mother he was after.

But because it was out of love he parades her to the leaders of the world without shame or hesitation. Wonders, strong feelings for someone can do. The pages of this book will not be enough for me to tell you the strange things people do in the name of love.

I remember my late dad once 'bundling us up and donating us' to our grandparents because he was so in love with a new woman that there was no longer room for us his children, in his heart. To ensure we were not interfering with his new found love he woke us up long before dawn one day, decades ago and gathered all our things as young children going on a holiday. He lied to his own children that we were going for a holiday at our grandparents, only for us to reach there and realise he was abandoning us for his new love and her children.

But for young people, you see someone you like and that desire for each other draws you closer to each other. You find ways to express that strong likening for each other until the man usually makes it official by proposing marriage or in the secular world officially ask to go on a date with you to get to know each other. In Christian circles, young people are expected to pray for God to fill in the blanks in knowing about each other's lives before you take a step of commitment or marriage. Hence the many churches which discourage dating or long courtships.

1 Corinthians 7:36 King James Version

36 But if any man think that he behaveth himself uncomely toward his virgin, if she pass the flower of her age, and need so require, let him do what he will, he sinneth not: let them marry.

You Will Need To Find More Reasons To Marry Along the Way

Once you become Mr. or Mrs that, you begin to 'see' more reasons for the way you feel about your and spouse wish you had married them earlier. You begin to think of the God you stood in front and promised to try your hardest to make this marriage work even in the best or worst conditions. You begin to think of the people you will disappoint if this 'marriage thing' failed after all the pomp and pageantry. You begin to think of the great environ you had or did not have and pray you can create same for your children. You also think of doing better than your parents did with their marriage if it was strong. You also begin to think of building a better marriage than your parents did, if they were divorced or their marriage was abusive. You get motivated by the fact that you want to repeat the beautiful marriage you saw your parents' display, if you are amongst the few who had this privilege of being raised in a healthy marriage. You might have married for love but once declared married, you will need more reasons than love to marry and marry well.

You Will Need To End With Commitment

Mark 10:8-9 King James Version

⁸ And they twain shall be one flesh: so then they are no more twain, but one flesh. ⁹ What therefore God hath joined together, let not man put asunder.

The ceremony the priest does on your wedding day is to legally and physically declare the two of you as having become one entity. The wedding ceremony most people spend their lives dreaming about or planning for only ensures your spouse and you become legally united. The marriage ceremony only blesses a union that has already been secured by the two families of the couple. It is the blessing of a union of two minds and hearts. Again, it is the blessing of an equal yoke between two God fearing people before many witnesses. The ceremony is not doing anything to you that the two of you have not agreed to do to each other before the marriage. It is not a spiritual portal that is suddenly going to transform you into the ideal wife or husband either.

NOW THAT YOU ARE MARRIED

Dear reader, I have taken my time to declare what marriage is so that we will stop attributing things to it that it cannot do by itself. Your wife's spirituality is not sexually transmittable. Neither is your husband commitment to the things of God something you can catch from being around him. But you can give birth to a child who is his split image because the two of you made the baby together physically.

However you cannot just become as anointed as he is just by being physically close to him. You will need to learn from what he does to build the relationship he has with God as his wife. Many women get disappointed that the men they married are not doing the spiritual activities they hoped they would do to get them to be as spiritual as they saw them to be before they proposed.

The two of you will become more united and exhibit similar behaviours when you commit to doing what will make each other happy. And the scriptures have already given clues as to what makes a wife or husband happy. Which is the fact that wives love to be loved in all situations whilst the husbands love to be respected or submitted to in all situations. Anything short of these and the couple will begin to see each other as the source of their problems instead of the solution. And begin to work at destroying the very union they work so had to contract.

Now that you are married understand that nothing short of a commitment to make that marriage work will make it work going forward.

PRAYER NUGGETS

You Will Need To Learn To Do Things For Reasons Other Than Your Feelings

1) If you are marrying the woman or man you want then you will have strong feelings for the person at the beginning of the relationship.
2) But as the relationship or marriage progresses you will need to find more reasons than passion to keep it going.
3) For a marriage or relationship to last, the couples will need to see love as a commitment and not just as a feeling.

CHAPTER 3

YOU WILL NOTICE YOUR SPOUSE HAS ADDICTIONS YOU DID NOT KNOW THEY HAD DURING COURTSHIP

Dealing With the Strong Desires of Youth

Romans 8:5-8 King James Version

^{5} For they that are after the flesh do mind the things of the flesh; but they that are after the Spirit the things of the Spirit. ^{6} For to be carnally minded is death; but to be spiritually minded is life and peace. ^{7} Because the carnal mind is enmity against God: for it is not subject to the law of God, neither indeed can be. ^{8} So then they that are in the flesh cannot please God.

Many times in Pentecostal circles when we were growing up in the 90s and early 2000s we heard people preach a lot on mortifying the desires of the flesh. You hear summons like that if you are fortunate to be in a living church. These days I hardly even hear anyone preach on such topics. But the danger of not touching on subjects like that is that it breeds Christians who have dual personalities. The one they bring to church and the one struggling to deal with the many desires which flood the heart of a young man or woman. Then there are the few preachers who have moved to the other extreme, where they only condemn the youth for having such immoral feelings or desires and never prescribe a remedy. Youth, hearing that kind of ministry live in condemnation and often lose their joy in the lord till they eventually backslide into the world.

Since preachers today have mostly decided not to deal with the elephant in the room i.e. the passionate desires of youth, I have decided to talk about it. Telling the youth to direct their attention to sports will not be enough to mitigate it. Because within sports other passions have also been awaken. Such as betting, alcoholism, drugs and hooliganism. There are others who are addicted to attention seeking habits and might have shared certain photos of themselves on the internet which could come back to haunt you after the marriage. The fine lady or gentleman you see today might have made some mistakes in the past which may come back to haunt them later in the marriage.

Hebrews 5:13-14 Amplified Bible

13 For everyone who lives on milk is [doctrinally inexperienced and] unskilled in the word of righteousness, since he is a spiritual infant. 14 But solid food is for the [spiritually] mature, whose senses are trained by practice to distinguish between what is morally good and what is evil.

It takes a matured Christian to marry the way marriage should be conducted. The bible defines a matured Christian as someone who has learnt to differentiate between right and wrong. A man or woman overcome with addiction does what will give him or her a fix whether it is right or wrong. The concept of right or wrong does not even come up in the decision making process of an addict to satisfy that uncontrollable desire.

Signs that Your Partner is An Addict before Marriage

Many spouses claim they had no clue concerning their partners' addiction before marriage. To ensure people pick on the right pointers. I have enumerated some common signs of hidden addiction. If you are courting someone and he shows these signs then it could be a pointer that your partner is having secrets addiction trouble through the following: 1) He or she will not be interested in participating in activities in church which mortify the flesh like praying in tongues for long hours, studying the bible on their own or even fasting; 2) He or she will have many secrets activities and interactions that will be kept from you as you prepare to get married. 3) They will often have friends or acquaintances they do not want you to meet. 4) Again they will make consistent expenditures and hide it from you or refuse to explain what it went into. 5) Your fiancé may earn income that they do not want you to know the source; 6) You will find them suddenly going on a spending spree but refusing to tell you how they came by the money; and 7) They would be found lying a few times about where they were, who they were with or what they were doing, as relationship progresses.

And dear reader, I am not talking about an unbeliever here or that guy that everyone knows to be unserious with the things of God. But a man or woman who is born again and is committed to going to church but has some dark secrets. People who are often seen as heroes in the community but are struggling with things when alone. It is more common than you think. Because I am sure you know people who are going through what I am talking about. I believe you saw it in your life or that of your friends and relatives but did not know what was at play in the marriage then. Many of the unresolved problems in marriages can be traced to addictions. Marriages are plagued by addictions more than anything else you can think off. Let us consider some addictions that may arise in marriages today.

Addiction to Substances

There are elders or deacons of churches, depending on the denomination who are smokers or alcoholics in secret. Some of these people had these addictions before conversion but fell back into them in their moments of weakness, as they went along their Christian lives but have since not been able to shake it off. Others also went back to their addictions because of the abuses they experienced in their marriages. There are spouses who fell back into gluttony because of depression and can no longer control their weight. Others have also chosen to make themselves happy by constant eating of sugary foods.

These addictions lead to the spouse's attention moving from the marriage unto them. Spending on these substances daily also lead to a waste of a lot of money a on these substances. Money badly needed for the family's maintenance or progress. Abusing these substances also lead to diseases in the future and may even end up reducing the quality of life of the spouse. The addict may lose appeal because he or she will always smell of alcohol or look obese. It can even end the marriage prematurely through protracted illness or even death of the addict.

Addictions to bad behaviour

There are spouses whose addicted behaviour will not show till you live with them in the same room as husband and wife. People who are addicted to never finishing what they start. Others are addicted to violence because they saw it growing up and after being born again they have still not been able to overcome that tendency. And though husband are mostly the culprits there are women who have been known to also strike their husbands with anything in hand when angry.

Others also destroy anything they lay their hands on when they are angry. And still others are obsessed with revenge whenever they are offended. Strangely there are husbands or wives who extend their anger to the children anytime they have a problem with their spouses. Then there are spouses with sex addiction: they cannot stay faithful to their spouse. Even worse are those who are attracted to unnatural sex or people of the same sex. Many Christian spouses have been shocked to see their spouses leave them for people of the same sex after years of marriage. It is usually an addiction they had which had not been resolved before entering the marriage.

Addiction to bad ideology or mind-set

Of all addictions which plague marriages nothing is more difficult to fight than the addiction to false ideology. Some time back in the Akan regions of Ghana, the prevailing ideology of irresponsible husbands was the fact that children belonged to the wives family, so the woman would benefit if they invested in them to become worthy in future. Another false ideology our fathers were addicted to was the fact that an African man was insufferably polygamous: so if you have a farm (wedded wife) you needed to have a garden (girlfriend).Unfortunately these devilish ideas still plague many marriages.

There are also wives with the false idea that their husbands should be taller than them. Such wives after marriage always become sad when they see picture of themselves with their husbands. The fact that they cannot look up to their husbands become an obsession till they are convinced they married the wrong man. And it does not matter even if he is the wisest man alive. There are still others who think a man should have more in everything than his wife and will therefore not feel comfortable in the marriage till the husband has attain more qualifications than they have. Though he might not be academically but business inclined. And still others, who believe till they have had a son or daughter they have not had children and will go through all kinds of humiliation to have that fixed.

Are all these not normal brother Alex, I can hear you dear reader asking, no they are not, they are addictions because we pursue these things without consulting God. They are addictions because they destroy the great things we already have but we still pursue them. They are addictions because it causes us to be bitter and ungrateful spouses who lose the affection of our spouses. Mostly after the spouse has fulfilled our dream for them they no longer want us, because of all the abuses we heaped on them to ensure they towed our line.

There are even others who destroy the ministry of their spouses because they had false ideologies on who a pastor is. Women who have the mind-set that no matter what they earn, it is the husband that must take care of every expense in the house whilst they spend their money on themselves and their family members alone.

PRAYER NUGGETS

Your Spouse Will Have Addictions You Did Not Notice During Courtship

1) You will notice your spouse has developed habits to cope with the strong desires of youth.
2) You will pick signs that your partner was an addict before Marriage.
3) Watch out for addictions to: bad ideologies or mind-sets; bad behaviours; and substance abuse.

CHAPTER 4

YOU WILL NOTICE YOUR SPOUSE KNOWS PEOPLE YOU WERE NOT AWARE OF DURING COURTSHIP

Proverbs 5:17-19 Amplified Bible

17 [Confine yourself to your own wife.] Let your children be yours alone, And not the children of strangers with you. 18 Let your fountain (wife) be blessed [with the rewards of fidelity], And rejoice in the wife of your youth.

The Example Of My Own Marriage

As I write you this chapter, a man is accused of disappearing the wife because he is said to have accused her of infidelity. This surprise that spouses get after marriage, especially when it concerns the spouse that is introvert, has destroyed many marriages. I always cringe when I hear young couple in love claiming they know everyone that the partner knows. Anytime I hear that I know there is a knowledge deficit which could 'grow to eat them up.' Because it is a relational impossibility to know everyone your spouse knows.

Because even if you were born in the same house or even born the same day you will not go to the same places at the same time all the time. And those different scenarios will expose you or your spouse to different kinds of people. But there is this tendency for spouses to think that somehow they should know everyone their partner knows or something fishy is going on. That is a lie from the devil: you and your spouse have a life time to know your friends and relatives. And there should be no rush about it whatsoever or you would accuse your spouse of things which do not exist.

I Met My Wife At Children Service

The first time I saw my wife, she was a teenager attending children service a.k.a Sunday school at a small assembly or branch of the Church of Pentecost we both attended together. Naturally we grew to know the same people because we operated essentially in the same circles. That is good and also not so good because we knew the good, the bad and the ugly about each other. But then went to different secondary schools so we built knew friendships, then to different universities so another new set of friends and acquaintances. Over the years as we date we came to know some of these friends in our respective secondary schools and universities.

But after school she moved to the UK I was in Ghana and there we met other people. By then we were courting but other friends came into the picture that were not mutual friends. People who tried to break our relationship or present themselves as better alternatives to me or her. After been married for over a decade she still does not know every friend or acquaintance I know and vice versa. Some I know by name when they occur in conversation, others I have only seen their pictures and still others by what they said at one point or the other.

Though we have over 300 mutual friends on Facebook and essentially share the same friends on other social media platforms. We do not know everyone that we each interact with. But those she interacts with often or those who become friends, I get to know them over time. If you have a friend and you do not want your spouse to know about him or her, then that is enough reason to break that friendship. Because believe it or not, every extra marital relationship starts with a client, an acquaintance or a friend.

People You May Not Know From School

You will not always know the acquaintances or even friends of your spouse because some of them will reach out to your partner years after they have completed school.

Some of those friendship might have gone comatose until they met at a meeting or in the office. Most time when such encounters are reported the other spouse do not take notice of it they are introduced to the person in person. So be opened to the idea that you will continually get to know people you did not know your spouse knew. It is part of the luxury marriage will afford over time even as you get to know your partner the more.

Distant Relatives You May Not Know

Believe you me even relatives who attend your marriage ceremony from your spouse's side you will not remember them afterwards. It will take years for you to meet them all if that is even possible in a place like Africa where we have such big extended families. There are family members who will be good to you, others will be indifferent and still others even hostile but remember who you married and focus on him or her instead. Now that you are married, understand that you will not stop encountering one kind of family member or the other you did not know through the various occasions the family will organise.

People From Church You May Not know

As a Christian couple some of the most influential people, as far as your marriage is concern will be people you befriend in church. Though you might be in the same church you may not make the same friends all the time. It is important to let your spouse know anyone who has become your friend because friends influence us more than we care to admit. Listen to your spouse if they say the sense or express some misgivings with your new found friend because it might be the caution you need to get out of a trap. Now that you are married ensure you attend the same church and assembly so your circle of influence will be shared by both of you.

People From Work You May Not Know

This is the tricky one, especially now that married people can reach work as early as 7:00am because of traffic after setting of from home around 5am and then get back home around 7pm with some of those same workers. You will realise that your spouse is spending more time at work than even at home. With time conversation will start in your absence and friendship will develop that you will not be part of. If you allow insecurity to take the better part of, you will start to dismiss any conversation which involves the new friend you are not comfortable with. Your spouse in order to keep such people from disturbing the peace at home will start keeping them off the radar, whilst still interacting with them.

The next thing you will realise is that he or she is picking ideas from such people without your input. Because what was discussed has not been brought to the house for you to correct wrong ideas and beliefs. Because work matters might not be discussed at home you will not notice when one co-worker is becoming prominent in your partner's life.

Now that you are married, make every effort to involve yourself in the activities of your spouse's workplace if possible. As people come to work at the workplace and clients come for services, it is normal that someone will try to start an inappropriate relationship with your spouse. Hence the needed to make yourself available from time to time at your spouse's workplace. So that your own spouse's co-workers and clients will help police him or her for you as you make friends with them. Now that you are married know that your partner is making new friends all the time and it is your responsibility to be there to make it with him or her.

PRAYER NUGGETS

You Will Notice Your Spouse Knows People You Were Not Aware Of During Courtship

1) Because your spouse might have attended schools you did not attend.
2) Because your spouse might have worked at a different place from yours.
3) Some of the people your spouse may know that you may not know may even be distant relatives or even former church members.

CHAPTER 5

YOU WILL NOTICE THAT THERE ARE SOME THINGS IN YOUR SPOUSES PAST YOU WERE NOT AWARE OF

Luke 8:17 Amplified Bible

17 For there is nothing hidden that will not become evident, nor anything secret that will not be known and come out into the open.

No One Likes An Unpleasant Surprise

I heard of the story of a woman who had lost the joy of her marriage and wanted to divorce her husband because of a nasty surprise she found about him some years into the marriage. This is because the husband, when they were courting told her he attended 'Tech'. The short form of what was then the University of Science and Technology in Kumasi the second city of Ghana. The woman who is a graduate from another university then assumed her husband was also a graduate. The husband to be at the time also made no effort to correct that wrong impression of him being a graduate. Then after the marriage, and it is always after the marriage that things settle enough for secrets to get revealed.

She realised all her husband's mates and acquaintances were not graduates and eventually gathered the courage to ask her husband why he had no records on his university education? To this, he asked her what university education? You asked me which school I attended and I said 'Tech', what I meant by that is Kumasi Secondary Technical School. I did not say I attended any university. The woman is still in shock as I write this chapter, because she taught she had married a graduate instead of a graduate of a technical secondary school. If the husband had been very opened about his educational background, perhaps it might not have mattered to her before the marriage. But now she feels trapped in a marriage she believes she was tricked into.

Spouses Believe They Marry People They Know Thoroughly

Essentially this is true but your spouse could not have told you everything about himself or herself. She could not have told you her first crush on a guy in the neighbourhood. Neither could she tell you all the things her siblings used to tease her with. Whiles it essential that the things which can affect your marriage are known, those which have nothing to do with the relationship should be on a need to know basis.

An example of things which your spouse does not need to know is how great your first boyfriend was to you or how good he made you feel. Your husband to be will be haunted by that information till he either breaks the engagement or until you find ways to convince him that he will not be playing second fiddle to his memory. This is especially true when your partner is a widow or widower: he or she respectively should be circumspect concerning what is shared about the previous relationship to avert situation where the new spouse feels like a second rate spouse.

Because the information you share of the previous relation can create the impression that you are not your true self in the current relationship. Constantly talking about things you did that you no longer do or things you said that you no longer say. Can create the impression that your previous relationship was better than the current one. And that there is more to you than you are exhibiting in the current relationship. He or she might think you are holding back because you still prefer the previous partner.

Now that you are married, be very circumspect concerning what you say about yourself, your parents or the mistakes of your past to your spouse because that information may distort your new spouse's knowledge of you as the relationship progresses. There are spouses who have been branded as being manipulative in their marriage whenever conflicts arise, because of things they told their spouses sometime in the past when they were courting. Examples of tales which may distort your spouse's view of you as you go into the future are stories on how you use to trick the many girls you dated as an unbeliever. In the good times of your relationship it with will elicit laughter but in times of conflict it will be cited as proof that you are deceiving her now.

Spouses Consider Keeping Secrets From Them As Manipulation

Ask any married person and they will tell you that if their partner kept information which could have affected their decisions to marry them then they have been deceived into the marriage. However couples, are reasonable enough to admit that even they, have not been able to share every tiny detail of their lives with their partner. Some things are not kept but simply forgotten until an issue or a traumatic experience brings it back from deep memory.

There are traumatic experiences that due to the pain and shame it caused your partner in the past, he or she might have pushed it into their sub conscious memory and forgotten about it. There are ladies who were raped by close family members and have never shared their experiences with anyone. An experience they might be too ashamed to discuss even after being born again. But such an experience can affect your attitude towards sex during the marriage so it is necessary to share it with your spouse to be without going into the gory details. Do not tell your spouse the number of sexual partners you might have had before being born again or during your state of backsliding. Neither create the impression you are a virgin when you are not.

One marriage ended right after honeymoon when the husband noticed his virgin wife was not a virgin after all. Let your spouse to be know that you are victorious Christians now, but you are not a virgin.

Do not hide behind scriptures like 'when you are born gain you are a new creator all things are passed away behold everything has become new' to rewrite your history. That fact that, you are no longer a virgin will not change because you got born again. You can only become a secondary virgin because you are now keeping your body pure for your husband.

You Do Not Need To Know Everything About Your Partner

I know many people find the above sub heading difficult to accept: because of how we often pride ourselves in how much we know our partners. Indeed couples feel much settled once they can predict the behaviour of their partners. Indeed, many ladies have lived with many unreasonable men without seeking for divorce because such men were thoroughly known to act that way.

A typical example comes to mind of a man I know who consistently disregarded his hard working wives advice and chose to speak ill of her at the slightest opportunity but is now living in a house she built after her pension. The interesting thing is that he built a house in his hometown despite the wives advice that the place is too remote for him to settle after retirement but as usual he ignored her. Only for him to go on retirement and acknowledge that she was right. But did his behaviour change after this? No it did not! His unreasonable behaviour and violent tendencies was known by everyone who knew the couple. Indeed he got away with 'murder' on many occasions. As I write this the wife has still not left him, though he is now living in her house as a retiree.

Many women have paid back their husband in 'a big way' for all the years of abuse they suffered when their husbands were in active service. This book will not be enough for me to recount the many marriages where the husbands as a young men did far less than this man but their Christian wives, when they went on retirement connived with their grown up kids to pay them back so severely that many died prematurely.

Why the difference, this woman of God adjusted her mind to the fact that she had married an unreasonable man and focused on raising her children. But other woman married men they thought were 'angels' for husbands, who later turned out to be the devil's incarnate. Hence their unresolved bitterness which they usually passed to even their children till the once highly revered 'demi god' husband and father becomes a byword when he is no longer sound economically.

Now that you are married you need to acknowledge the fact that you will not know everything about your partner from the beginning of the marriage. That is why you have a lifetime to fine out all you need to know about him or her. Encourage each other as a new couple to avoid keeping secret information which can affect the family. Keeping secrets which can affect your family will never allow your spouse to know you well enough to be of effective help to you.

That secret you are keeping will become a filter through which all your communications will go through. That secret will inform your actions and arguments but your spouse will never understand you because he or she will not know what you know.

PRAYER NUGGETS

You Will Notice That There Are Some Things In Your Spouses Past You Were Not Aware Of

1) If you have a secret that can affect someone's decision to marry you, it is not right to keep it to yourself because no one likes an unpleasant surprise.
2) Because most spouses consider keeping secrets which could have affected their decision to marry you, from them as manipulation.
3) However you do not need to know everything about your partner to love them.

CHAPTER 6

YOU WILL SUDDENLY BECOME AWARE OF WEAKNESSES YOU DID NOT KNOW YOU HAVE

Romans 7:18-25 Amplified Bible

18 For I know that nothing good lives in me, that is, in my flesh [my human nature, my worldliness—my sinful capacity]. For the willingness [to do good] is present in me, but the doing of good is not. 19 For the good that I want to do, I do not do, but I practice the very evil that I do not want. 20 But if I am doing the very thing I do not want to do, I am no longer the one doing it [that is, it is not me that acts], but the sin [nature] which lives in me. 21 So I find it to be the law [of my inner self], that evil is present in me, the one who wants to do good. 22 For I joyfully delight in the law of God in my inner self [with my new nature], 23 but I see a different law and rule of action in the members of my body [in its appetites and desires], waging war against the law of my mind and subduing me and making me a prisoner of the law of sin which is within my members. 24 Wretched and miserable man that I am! Who will [rescue me and] set me free from this body of death [this corrupt, mortal existence]? 25 Thanks be to God [for my deliverance] through Jesus Christ our Lord! So then, on the one hand I myself with my mind serve the law of God, but on the other, with my flesh [my human nature, my worldliness, my sinful capacity—I serve] the law of sin.

We Marry People Focusing On Their Strength

Due to our often outspoken parents and relatives everyone grows up having an idea of their weaknesses. People often choose spouses who can best address their weaknesses.

This, young people do mostly consciously or unconsciously sometimes. I remember watching some ladies answering the question of 'what do you look out for in a man'. To my surprise, most of them wanted men who will cover their weaknesses. One said she wanted a man who could pray because she is lazy when it comes to prayer. Another said she wanted a man who is tall because she is short. Another said, her family is poor so she needs a man of substance so he can help get her out of her poverty stricken life.

Knowing your weakness as a young unmarried person is very important because it can affect your choice of a spouse. It can also affect your appeal to your potential suitor. Many ladies have lost the chance to be with the man of their dreams because they were perceived by them to be unruly. It is very easy for a woman to be seen as cantankerous or argumentative if she speaks her mind without the emotional maturity or strength to know when to do that and when to keep her cool. So a woman who cannot control her tongue may invest her life and heart into a man who may never consider her a marriage material. Because she will be seen by him as someone who is not submissive.

Most men do not like engaging in arguments. Because men are less able, when it comes to talking as compared to women. Therefore most men see it as a weakness when a woman has the propensity to say what she feels. Indeed the easiest way to deceive a man into marriage is to hold your piece as a woman in the face of extreme provocation. Ask most men about their now troublesome spouse and they are most likely than not, to tell you their wives were the quite submissive type when they were dating or courting. In fact, ask any man who cannot stand going home because of a quarrelsome wife and they will, if they can remember tell you that one day in their marriage their quiet, submissive wife, announced that she was no longer going to keep quite. Anytime you hear that statement from a woman prepared for trouble.

Now that you are married you will notice you have weaknesses that you have not paid attention to, sometimes for years.

Weaknesses From Your Temperament

Since the time of Moses introverts have been seen by others as not being go getters or strong leaders. They are seen as being weaklings because they do not tell people their mind immediately things happen. I remember right after marriage, my wife who had this perception of me, advised me 'to be strong because I am now the head of a family'. I did not know I was weak till she gave me that advice just a day after marriage. I remember turning towards her and saying 'the gentle strides of a leopard is not to be mistaken as a sign of cowardice but strategy'. In the same way since she has a strong personality she is accustomed to getting her way as she was growing up. So I had to let her know at the early stage of the marriage that she is fond of giving people pressure when she wants things done but she does not apply the same attitude to herself when she is needed to get thing done.

That candour from the both of us helped us survive a turbulent first two years of marriage. Now that you are married you will hear from your spouse complaining about the weaknesses of your temperament. From experience, when your spouse makes those observations, it could off lead to self-doubt or fights. However do not be too defensive neither consider it as a condemnation of your personality because no one is as invested in your life as your spouse is. Hence their constant scrutiny of what you do and how you do it.

Weaknesses From Your Upbringing

Now that you are married, you will notice you have weaknesses occasioned by your upbringing. No matter how refined you think you are, your parents did not bring you up to do everything to please your husband or wife.

Listen to this illustration of my point in the form of a story I once heard of a marriage which almost ended before it was even one day old. The MC of a wedding reception called for advice from the family as is customarily done in Ghana. So the groom's mother took the microphone and talked about how well they had trained their son. Then the mother of the bride also took the microphone after she was done and extolled the virtues they had instilled in their daughter.

Before the father of the groom could join in what was fast becoming a contest of 'we are a better family than our in-laws' the pastor intervened. He admonished the two parents to focus on the family their children are going to build as newlyweds instead of the ones they are coming from. Because even they as couples of many years, are aware they are not perfect so how can they raised a perfect children? A case in point in my marriage, I did not know, I did not enjoy eating together anyone, not even with my own wife until I got married. Because as kids we were always given food in separate plates. Any time my wife wanted us to eat from the same bowl I would struggle with it. I did not know I had that weakness till I got married. I believe if you are married, you are also noticing similar things happening in your marriage.

Weaknesses From Your Acquired Habits

If there is a thing fighting against many marriages more than any other thing then it will be weaknesses coming out of acquired bad habits. Most especially bad habit acquired during adulthood. Habits acquired to manage our lusts. Habits carried out in secret to help us deal with the loneliness of single life. Habits acquired through experimentations with our bodies and the curiosity to know new things, which later become addictions. I know of people who were introduced to masturbation because they were watching tutorials on how to control premature ejaculation. Masturbation is a great weakness that can plague marriages. Because it can lead to insatiable desire for sex.

The lack of enjoyment of sex with your partner and even addiction to pornography because you need a stimulant to keep it going. Now that you are married you will realise pornography addiction is a great weakness because you spouse will never be as stimulating as those adult industry professionals are trained to be. You will realise that your spouse does not put you in the mood as much as those videos. And for those who went the line of masturbation to deal with sexual sins you will notice your spouse does not satisfy you as those objects or your own self stimulation. You will notice your spouse feeling he or she is competing with that act of masturbation to satisfy you. Your spouse will lose respect for you as someone involved in unclean activities though on the outside you present yourself as a victorious Christian.

You will notice that due to the lack you might have experienced when growing up, your attitude towards money especially how is always bringing conflict. Again you will notice that, if you were brought up in a rich home your attitude towards money and how it is spent may bring conflict between you and your spouse because you may spend beyond his or her expectation. Because you come from affluence you will not see that behaviour as a weakness till you marry and have to make your own money.

Now that you are married your spouse will notice several weaknesses in your life. Do not panic, your spouse is not being unreasonable, you are just being watched more closely than ever before. In your family you most likely had other siblings so you were monitored but not with the intensity that a loved one would. Because every action of yours affects them directly. When we notice our weaknesses, let us work on them so the lessons we learn can be shared with others. It is from my own experiences of discovering my weaknesses that has informed the writing of this chapter.

PRAYER NUGGETS

You Will Suddenly Become Aware Of Weaknesses You Did Not Know You Have

1) You will suddenly realise you had weaknesses you did not know you had because there is now someone close to your heart enough to trigger them.
2) We mostly marry people focusing on their strength whilst busily explaining every negative thing we see with them.
3) But everyone has weaknesses because of: upbringing; temperament and acquired habits.

CHAPTER 7

YOU WILL BECOME AWARE OF STRENGTHS YOU DID NOT KNOW YOU HAVE

1 Peter 3:6-8 Amplified Bible

6 just as Sarah obeyed Abraham [following him and having regard for him as head of their house], calling him [a]lord. And you have become her daughters if you do what is right without being frightened by any fear [that is, being respectful toward your husband but not giving in to intimidation, nor allowing yourself to be led into sin, nor to be harmed].7 In the same way, you husbands, live with your wives in an understanding way [with great gentleness and tact, and with an intelligent regard for the marriage relationship], as with [b]someone physically weaker, since she is a woman. Show her honour and respect as a fellow heir of the grace of life, so that your prayers will not be hindered or ineffective.

The Things We Accommodate Now

When we were growing up we often heard this counsel from successfully married men and women 'never take advice from single people concerning how to conduct your marriage because they will not understand what you are going through.' Getting married has taught me that this saying is really true. I have had to advice an unmarried friend to not behave like he is an expert on marriage. Because marriage can truly be understood by those who are married. He ignored my advice and ended up trying to break the very marriage he initially thought of saving. What am I saying? Marriage changes people. So no matter what you read about marriage, it will not make you better at marriage, till you actually practise it. Marriage has transformed the once lazy girls before marriage into dutiful wives. It has even transformed international high fliers into stay at home moms and dads.

I remember once hearing that one of our brothers' marriages has gone four years without children. As a bachelor I was sure I would not be able to keep my marriage if we were childless for that long. I was sure the longest I could take that challenge was three years. Yet by the grace of God I was faithful to my wife all the nine solid years we were trying for a child. Strength which could have only come from the grace of God for married people. This is why another word for grace is favour. Thus the bible says 'he who finds a wife obtains favour or grace from the Lord!'

Strength From The Love of Your Spouse

There are things you swore as a single person that you would not tolerate from a spouse but you will find yourself accommodating even more. It is not because you are a full but that your love spouse so much that you are ready stomach many of their excesses. Sometime it not because your spouse is doing anything bad but the fact that you have to give up so much to be able to live with him or her. There are spouses who have not spoken to some close family members for years because they chose to marry the person they are with now.

People they believed, they will not be able to live without speaking to them for so long but are now doing it because of the strength that comes from truly loving someone. For the unmarried, one of the key ways to know if you love someone enough to marry them. Is to assess if you are ready to sacrifice for them to be happy. If you have no inclination to sacrifice to be with them then you like them but are yet to love them. Now that you are married you should look forward to making sacrifices to see the relationship work.

Strength From The Love of Your Children

Many mothers are heroes in the eyes of their children because they exhibit this strength a lot. It is one of the major reasons why mother's days is so much better than father's days. Father's especially those of my father's generation hardly separated their children from their wives when it came to rejection. Most if your mother was not favoured then you the child was out of luck. If your mother was pushed out of the marriage, then you had to go with her and all things concerning you were mostly forgotten. In my own experience my father actually after dating another women gathered all our things and went to dump us by the road side. He then told us, his own children because of the other woman he was seeing, to go to our grandparents because he no longer wanted us.

But women often get the strength to endure a lot of abuse from marriage because of the children. My mother endured a lot from my dad whenever he found another woman because she was sure he would not look after us if she left him. There are other women who have stayed with abusive men because they did not want to have children from different men. There are also, upstanding men who deal with the worst of bosses and work under some of the most difficult of circumstances because they want to provide for their children. Now that you are married you will often hear in your heart 'be careful what you do does not affect the children negatively'. Please consider it carefully because you might be the beneficiary of another mother's decision to put you above her needs in the past.

Strength From Your Upbringing

There are people who are brought up to be strong. Either due to the fact that they are survivors of constant abuse or that they had to live under extreme poverty. There poor had to mostly go through life believing God for even the smallest of things. Above all they had to struggle for things other people take for granted. That kind of upbringing if well harnessed can make a spouse extremely grateful and appreciative of what a better endowed wife or husband respectively is doing for him or her. There are married woman and even men who have endured so much from their spouses because they paid for the schooling or even brought them to the city.

I know of a married woman who had the strength to endure so much from her husband over the years because he was the one who initially gave her the seed capital for her thriving business. Others have developed great strength to make marriages work with an unwilling and uncooperative spouse because they saw their mother or father do it when they were growing up.

I know of a married woman who at the initial stage of her marriage had to give her car to her husband whilst she boarded commercial vehicles to ensure that marriage was saved. And it worked because they are still married ten years on with lovely children. I believe as an unmarried woman, there is no way this wife would have thought she would have the strength to make such sacrifices for her marriage. Now that you are married you will realise you are doing everything possible to have a marriage like your parents or one that is opposite to what they had.

Strength From Your Temperament

There are tendencies we have or were born with. I have watched my twin daughters from day one and have been left in no doubt that temperaments are things you are born with. Because from 'day one' one has shown to be an introvert and the other an extrovert. As they grow up, those traits are becoming more crystallised as their personality form along those lines.

In marriage our temperaments can feed into the strengths we have to deal with certain difficulties better. Introvert oriented spouses especially, are able to keep the difficulties in their marriage from even their best friends or even their parents for years. This could give spouses the breathing space to resolve whatever difficulties they might be having.

Others have used their ability to start friendship easily to help their spouses secure contracts or even employment. Through their extensive network of an extrovert spouse many introvert partner have been able to secure political offices.

Every spouse is a suitable partner to his or her spouse, hence whatever strengths your temperament affords you, use it to push your partner and your marriage forward. One woman on Pentv. Thus, Pentecost Television Ghana's M'awareɛ (or My marriage in English) remarked that, she enjoyed seeing couples fighting because that was all she saw when she was growing up. So after getting married she found herself provoking the husband severally in order to start a fight. But the husband's calm introvert personality will not indulge her.

She did her possible best to starts fights but on each occasion her husband's calm non combative temperament thwarted her efforts, until she gradually understood that marriage can be done without frequent fights. Here the husband temperament help her change from a cantankerous wife to and understand one. Now that you are married understand that there are some strengths you have by reason of your temperament that your husband or wife does not have and use it to push the marriage forward.

PRAYER NUGGETS

You Will Become Aware Of Strengths You Did Not Know You Have

1) You will with each difficulty or challenge in the marriage become of strengths you did not know you have.
2) Strength emanating from the love your spouse, children and even your parents.
3) Strength from your temperament, upbringing and your faith in God.

CHAPTER 8

YOU WILL DEAL WITH ISSUES YOU NEVER HAD BEFORE IN YOUR LIFE

Ecclesiastes 3:11 Amplified Bible

God Set Eternity in the Heart of Man

11 He has made everything beautiful and appropriate in its time. He has also planted eternity [a sense of divine purpose] in the human heart [a mysterious longing which nothing under the sun can satisfy, except God]—yet man cannot find out (comprehend, grasp) what God has done (His overall plan) from the beginning to the end.

Introduction

As a young man or woman you definitely had issues growing up. Issues with passing your examinations well enough to get the courses and schools you desired. If very talented you excelled in extra curricula activities like sports. We may have even worried about how to live as an admirable person in society. Then there were times we desired as young adults to live well enough to please our parents or guardians. We might even have dealt with issues of how to handle friends and their way word ways. We might have had issues concerning how we look compared to others as teens. Or issues with how to live a victorious life as a new convert in Christ. Then others had issues with choosing a life partner or handling courtship in righteousness.

But there are issues which arise only after you are married. These are the issues we will be discussing in this chapter. We need to talk about this before you begin to think as a young spouse that your marriage has too many issues to deal with. Remember a great miracle took place when you got married. Because you suddenly had the desire to stay with another person. Not minding the fact that you will share everything including your bed with him or her. Think about that for a second!

Let us consider the many odd things that you goggle together as a young couple. Before you married, you met an adult you did not grow up with but somehow felt connected to. Someone who is not a relative of yours in any shape or form but you felt drawn to. Someone who is a member of the opposite sex and might even have a different temperament from yours but you bonded with. With these differences mentioned above it is extremely naïve for young couples to often expect to have an issue free marriage.

Knowing this you will understand that it is extreme optimism that makes the daunting task of marriage, seem so easy and desirable. Every worthwhile endeavour like marriage succeeds spite of challenges or difficult issues and not because there were none. Let the storms you see in your marriage strengthen you to offer value to others in similar situations. Now that you are married you will deal with issues you might not have dealt with before as a single person.

Issues with In-laws

There are many people who grow up experiencing the love of their parents. People who were praised for everything they did. People who were seen as special because they were name after their beloved grandmother or grandfather. These people marry and an in laws only sees them as competition for scarce resources from their son. Again there are sons who are revered in their families but marry into families where the in-law believes their daughter has married someone beneath them. Women who thoughts they were assets to any man they will marry till their in-laws made them aware that they are parasites or gold diggers in their estimation. People who were hardly making ends meet till they married a rich man's daughter and were transformed into managers of big companies overnight.

Son-in-law who have risen from obscurity to become high fliers who now have to goggle managing a fast growing business and satisfying a well accomplish father or mother in law. You may think such a person is lucky but there are people in this situation who are under extreme stress on a daily basis.

Issues with Children

Most of us are eager to have children when we marry because we know having children brings problems but not having children bring even worse problems. Most of us want children because they will care for us when we are older. Even if we are rich to take care of ourselves in old age we want children to continue our legacy or keep our blood line alive. But sometimes a wife conceives for nine months and instead of giving birth to a healthy child gives birth to a child who cannot be trained for the things above because they are not healthy. No couple ever thinks they will give birth to a child or children who will depend on them for ever. Children who have your name but cannot take it anywhere because they cannot even fend for themselves.

Now that you married, you need to pray that all your children will be healthy enough to carry your name far. Now that you are married you need to pray so your children do not drag you to places of trouble you never thought you would ever go. Because there are children whose actions have bankrupted their parents and sent others to prison. There are God fearing parents who have never aborted a pregnancy in their lives but have had to do it for a child or two. Now that you are married, pray that your children will always lead you to a place of wealth or honour and not a place of dishonour or disgrace.

Issues with where to stay

I know a lady who married a young guy and in just three years into the marriage his firm decided to relocate him to the United

States of America. This young wife never thought of making a home in the United States yet marriage has sent her to that very place. A place where she will stay for most of her life. In contrast marriage has taken some couples to remote areas the never thought they would stay. I visited a young pastor friend on mission field who house initially had no ceiling or flooring. Before ministry this young man was a consulted who had married a well-travelled wife who is accustomed to the fine things of life. But immediately her husband was called into the ministry she had to give up this lifestyle. For a life in a rural area so remote that their child could not even find an appropriate school to attend.

Now that you are married, pray that the lord will lead your family where ever they go so you will be prepared for whatever challenges that place my bring to you in particular and the family in general. Now that you are married you may stay in a place you do not like or with people who irritate you. All of these are unforeseen issues you will deal with as a spouse.

Issues with where to worship

In Ghana mostly, the wedding is done at the girl's place of worship as a sign that she is now joining the husband at his place of worship. Even within the same church different congregations might have different cultures or approaches to life. The young lady then have to sometimes deal with many of the things she is not used to at the husband place of worship. I remember as a member of the church of Pentecost, having to enter a church, most of us never thought we would enter because it started as a church involved idol worship. Growing up we heard the founder went for an idol from Nigeria and built the church around it.

But marriage took us there because the fiancé of one of our church members attended church there. So we had to have the wedding there because she was one of their very best members. She is now a committed member of our church, doing exploits for the lord through her singing ministry. I do not believe, until she was engage to our member she ever thought of worshipping with us. In fact, she even thought we will not attend the wedding because of how the church started.

But we could see the church had undergone a Pentecostal transformation after the founder's death. There are wives whose husbands broke away from the main church and they had to move into a classroom for worshipped after doing most of their worship in a state of the arts auditorium. Now that you are married, pray that where you worship with your family helps you as a wife or husband to live for Christ.

PRAYER NUGGETS

You Will Deal With Issues You Never Had Before In Your Life

1) Marriage introduces variables in a spouse's life, which were never there before: husband, children, in-laws etc.
2) Issues with where to stay, such that it will be convenient for husband and wife.
3) Issues with where to worship if the husband and wife are both prominent in their churches or assemblies.

CHAPTER 9

YOU WILL NEED TO MAKE ROOM IN YOUR HEART AND MIND TO ACCOMMODATE YOUR SPOUSE

Ephesians 5:22-33 New International Version

22 Wives, submit yourselves to your own husbands as you do to the Lord. 23 For the husband is the head of the wife as Christ is the head of the church, his body, of which he is the Saviour. 24 Now as the church submits to Christ, so also wives should submit to their husbands in everything.25 Husbands, love your wives, just as Christ loved the church and gave himself up for her 26 to make her holy, cleansing[a] her by the washing with water through the word, 27 and to present her to himself as a radiant church, without stain or wrinkle or any other blemish, but holy and blameless.

You will Need To Accommodate Your Spouse's Ignorance

There are things you take for granted because you grew up a man or woman that your spouse has no knowledge of. A friend of mine shared with me some years ago, a situation between him and his wife which illustrates the shocking ignorance that highly intelligent and exposed spouses sometimes show in marriage. His wife who learnt how to drive some years before he did, called him in the early days when she was transferred to join him in the city where he works. Let me dear reader, make it abundantly clear that she was driving without any trouble in the busiest city in Ghana before she come to this city which is fourth in size compared to the first one she came from. She called him one fine morning to asked which exist she should take out of the round about which leads to her workplace. A journey he had made with her on several occasions for several months.

Another friend of mine also shared with me the shocking story of her husband calling her all the way from Europe, only to ask her how to fry an egg. She was shocked that something as easy as frying an egg her beloved husband was still not up to it. The bible talks about couples submitting to one another so we can learn from each other what we do not know or are not aware of in life.

You Will Need To Accommodate Your Spouse's Weaknesses

I once read that David Beckham the former England international's wife now has to check him from buying a new car every time he goes out. Imagine having a weakness for expensive cars! If such a weakness is not checked you will soon run out of money or space to store them. David did not have this weakness when he started playing football years ago, but as his endorsements increased and his ability to buy the most exotic vehicles increased it became a weakness. I am sure the wife has weakness of her own but it is certainly not in buying expensive cars. I also watched a documentary which showed a wife obsessed with expensive hand bags. Some of them so expensive that it could buy a good car! She was able to keep this habit up because she ordered for them without paying for it with her own money. Imagine the outrage it could cause the husband if he paid attention to the fortune that she spends on this habit of buying expensive hand bags.

Many couples fail to deal with the weaknesses which become prominent as the marriage progresses. Unfortunately most spouses react to these weaknesses instead of respond to them. Most spouses usually view these emerging weaknesses as a sign that the husband or wife is changing for the worse. This reaction is often met with opposition from the partner because mostly the spouse complaining equally has weaknesses that he or she is not dealing with.

You Will Need To Accommodate Your Spouse's Needs

Your beautiful wife has needs, it is a reality that men often come to know in a relationship. There is an adage in Ghana that 'if you are dating a women and she tells you about her needs or difficulties: she is only telling you the problems you will be helping her solve in the future'. Most often than not the men appear in relationships as heroes or invincible to their women because of all the sacrifices they make to please them. Most women therefore get overwhelmed with the many needs surrounding their newly married husband. Because after marriage men relax and also desire to be taken care of by their wives. There is no human on earth who has no needs. Take note, I did not say wants but needs, we all have needs tied to our location, profession, upbringing, education, calling and relations.

If you are in a relationship and you still do not know the needs of our partner it means you do not know him or her enough. Most people in relationships are so overwhelmed by the strengths of their partner that they neglect to prepare for their needs. For some spouses they need to be supported financially for a long time though they are the heads of the house. Others need you the husband to take care of young children because they are on night duties. Other spouses needs a partner who will be frequenting the hospital because of a diseases they are battling with. Still other spouses by nature need their partners to live without them for long periods of time because of the nature of their jobs or their professions. Others have needs which have resulted from their addictions and they expect their spouses to help them deal with it.

Now that you are married, you need to prepare yourself to deal with the needs of your spouse. Failure to do so will lead to your partner seeing you as a problem instead of a helper. It is from this truth that God made Eve as a help meet and not just a soul mate. The focus of modern relationships on having a soul mate instead of a help mate is the reason many relationships and marriages are struggling. Everyone who marries has needs whether they are conscious of it or not and expect their spouses to help them meet those needs. When spouses fail to do that, it leads to disenchantment, bitterness, loss of affection, loveless marriages and subsequently separation or divorce.

You Will Need To Accommodate Your Spouse's Family Members

An African adage says 'we do not marry an individual but a family' Failure to appreciate the wisdom of this saying has led many spouses to take steps to antagonise the family of their spouses. There is a good reason why during the marriage ceremony family members were present as witnesses to what transpired. Interestingly the family of your wife or husband are not only physically interested in the marriage but spiritually interested too. Additionally it takes the witches in your family to allow the spirits from outside the family to attack you. Call it witchcraft studies 101, the law of witchcraft and sorcery says 'a man enemies are the people of his or her household.' Hence the way you treat the families behind your marriages goes a long way to determine whether you have blissful or battlefield marriages.

Tapping from the issue of addressing spousal needs as discussed above, let us consider this: there are spouses who are the bread winners of their families. Once you marry them, you should be ready to help them continue in that role or risk turning their former dependents into your enemies. But once you please family members you get the benefit of the good ones becoming guards for your property, babysitters for your children, cooks for your family, confidants and allies to help you keep your spouse. Unfortunately bad family members if not properly supervised can steal your things, defile your children, and assist your spouse to cheat on you or even encourage him or her to divorce or separate from you.

Now that you are married one of your roles now is to help your spouse play a beneficial role in his or her family. You have formed a new family with him or her but that has not taken your spouse from the original family you took them from. Indeed in most traditional setting, how beneficial your spouse is to his or her family will show if you are a good husband or wife. Spouses, especially wives are treated badly during the funeral rites of their late husband if she is seen as the reason their son or brother refused to be of help to them whilst he was alive. Young wife reading this, you are duly notified.

PRAYER NUGGETS

You Will Need To Make Room In Your Heart And Mind To Accommodate Your Spouse

1) For the marriage to work, you will need to make room in your heart and mind for your spouse.

2) You will need to make room in your heart and mind to accommodate your spouse's ignorance of some things you take for granted.

3) You will need to accommodate your spouse's needs and that of his or her family when required to do so for peace and harmony to prevail.

CHAPTER 10

YOU WILL NOTICE THAT THERE WILL BE THINGS YOU WILL COMPLAIN ABOUT BUT YOUR SPOUSE WILL BE UNABLE TO STOP

1 Corinthians 6:12 King James Version

12 All things are lawful unto me, but all things are not expedient: all things are lawful for me, but I will not be brought under the power of any.

Your husband or wife, because he or she respectively was brought up to believe, there are things her or she will be punished for doing and others that they could get away with, will develop bad habits because there was no punishment for those acts. I have a saying I usually tell young couples when they visit after their wedding to thank me for attending. What I usually tell a new couple is that 'you cannot change what you accommodate.' That if you truly want something changed, you will have to insist on it till it is done.

One of the greatest challenges of living with a loved one comes from not liking something they do whilst not having the courage to complain about it to his or her face. Because if an obvious wrong goes on for long without challenge, over time that seed will infect the offended party, who will consciously or unconsciously grow wrong habits or attitudes to counter that of the offending spouse. Now that you are married you will observe that with or without malice intended there are some bad habit or attitudes that despite your consistent complaints your spouse will not be able to stop completely.

How Your Spouse Interacts With His or Her Family

One of the difficult things to change about a spouse is how he or she interacts with the family. Some spouses will tend to meet every need of their family because they were the bread winners before they married. Attempts to remind them that they have their own family now so they should concentrate on using their limited resources on them instead can lead to all kinds of resistance. There are spouses who also had grudges with members of their family before marriage and will not listen to their new spouse to make amends no matter how much they plead. An unwise spouse might think that not sharing with the spouse's family might benefit them.

Forgetting that if siblings he or she grew up with or parents who gave birth to him or her cannot be forgiven, how much more they who were strangers that they met and married when they offend them? There are husband who put their parents and sibling needs even above that of their wives. Forgetting that these people were there but they still saw the need to marry their spouse. Let me give you an example I witnessed myself. And it was the wife of a relative who had been complaining about his tendency to choose his family over and above her needs. She had waited for more than three years after the marriage but had still seen no change in his attitude. I was therefore not surprised when the marriage fell on the rocks in spite of the children they shared.

The man who chose a fridge over his unborn child

A wife lamented to me bitterly about how her husband's quest to send his sister's fridge to be repaired resulted in her being left in labour at home for a long time. Because the husband left her with the choice of finding a commercial vehicle to convey her to the hospital. After several hours of an agonizing search for a commercial vehicle she found one. Because their only car was out of the house conveying her husband sister's fridge to a repair shop. She had several other examples where the husband seem to constantly choose his family over her. No wonder that marriage broke down eventually in spite of the three children it produced. Because the husband was unable to scale back the extent of his involvement or participation in addressing issues concerning individual members of his extended family after marriage.

Now that you are married the bible says you the man shall leave your family and be cleaved to your spouse so that what was once two individuals can now become one flesh.

How Your Spouse Interacts With His or Her Friends

There are people who cannot scale back the extent of their involvement with their friends even after they are married. People who can come home after eleven in the night because they went out with friends who might still be single to celebrate one thing or the other. Even if your spouse was once part of these friends your spending so much time with them outside the house will offend them.

Because anytime you spend with others no matter what you call them, is time you spend away from him or her. There are spouses who feel very comfortable coming home late in the night very often because it is a habit they acquired during their singlehood and are finding it difficult to adjust to their new married situation. That is how unhealthy relationships at work start. That is also how married people manage to avoid dealing with issues at home by hiding at work.

The Wife Who Left Home To Attend To A Political Party Meeting

There first day I head of a wedding during the weekday was this couple's marriage. They had dated for a while as co-workers in different departments and eventually decided to marry. But soon after the man went on retirement, we began to hear the marriage was on the rocks. The wife who was a very active political party activists before marriage had continued without scaling back her political party's activities even after having a child.

Listening to the husband, she could sometime leave her husband for days to attend rallies and sort, in spite of his constant complaints. The husband who was far older than her and had lost the privileges he had as a worker could do nothing as sometimes young men from the party came to pick her from their house. Imagine the headache this man had gone through seeing his wife picked by young men whose character he could not vouch for. The marriage eventually broke down.

Now that you are married, you need to realise that when you say home, it refers to only one specific place. Again you need to understand that home is not your parents' house, your best friend's house nor your workplace but the house you share with your wife or husband and or children.

Some Bad Behaviours of Your Spouse

Spouses are mostly well behaved, that is why we marry them. But if you court for someone for a long time, you will soon realise that for every three strengths that you partner has he or she may exhibit one character or attitude you do not like or feel comfortable with. There are ladies who have kept their virtues i.e. they are virgins but when offended will speak so rudely or profanely that you would wonder whether they were raised in a Christian home.

This reason is why so many long courtships do not end up in marriage. But contrary to popular belief, this occasional show of bad character is not because the person is pretending but because you see less of each other compared to the way you would, if you were staying together as a couple. Hence it appearing like it is occasional instead of a routine behaviour he or she exhibits when the conditions are right.

Indeed all of us exhibit the character our parents allowed us to have. Or better still we exhibit a combination of our mom and dad's characters. But if born again, we exhibit the character we have allowed the Holy Spirit working with our human spirits to produce as fruit in our flesh. So in spite of how we behave, it is as a result of a long process of pain, convenience, mischief and the fear of God.

So love may blind those who meet strangers and after a short courtship marry them. But those who marry their friends, work colleagues and church mates know, that loving is knowing what your fiancé's strengths and weaknesses are before the marriage. Bearing in mind that whatever faults you see before the marriage will grow after the marriage because of proximity and frequent interactions.

Bath Twice Or I will divorce You

For most men not bathing twice is not such a big deal to us. But after marriage we cease to live alone and start to share intimacy: a bedroom and bed with a woman, how we smell in the night ceases to be a trivial matter. A pastor once shared an experience he had with a couple. The wife was bent on leaving the man though she is a Christian. Initially the pastor thought it was because the man was not performing in bed, an issue that is very difficult to deal with from his experience. But when the lady confided in him he realised the man is a hard worker and so comes home from work sweating profusely.

However he has, despite months of complaining refused to bath in the evening before coming to bed. The problem has become so overwhelming that she had decided to leave her matrimonial home. At his juncture the pastor heaved a sigh of relief that it was not something more serious and told the wife to relax. He then called the husband alone and instructed him 'to go and bath in the night to avoid losing your marriage. He then added 'do you know the kind of things men who come here have to stop to keep their marriages? If you think bathing twice in a day is hard so you will let your marriage break then think about this.

Do you know what the new wife who will come will want you to stop if this one leaves you? That I assure may be something far harder for you to do than this. Besides she has offered to prepare hot water for you every evening.' However it is not only men who are guilty of not wanting to bath twice: I also know of a woman whose husband was threating to leave her because she has refused to bath in the evening.

Now that you are married understand that your body no longer belongs to you alone but your husband or wife. This does not only apply to sex alone but also to how clean or healthy it is kept. No husband will be happy with a wife who eats at odd hours neither will a wife be happy with a husband who hides and takes destructive drinks or substances into his body. Because when the repercussions come the spouse will not bear it alone.

PRAYER NUGGETS

There Will Be Things You Will Complain About But Your Spouse Will Be Unable To Stop

1) How your spouse interacts with his or her family might not change though you complain about it.
2) Your spouse might not be able to stop certain behaviours because it is an addiction.
3) Your spouse might not change the way they interact with their friends though you complain about it.

CHAPTER 11

YOU WILL HAVE OPPORTUNITIES YOU NEVER HAD BEFORE

Proverbs 18:22 King James Version

22 Whoso findeth a wife findeth a good thing, and obtaineth favour of the Lord.

The scripture above is very revealing because it is not talking about finding a beautiful woman but about finding a wife. This can be interpreted in many ways: that finding a woman who is a wife material is because you are favoured of the lord; it can also mean that there is a favour from the lord that comes upon you once you find a wife. But I am more inclined to the rendering of the latter. Because Bible version after version used the conjunction 'and' and not 'during' or 'before' you find a wife. So the favour from the lord comes because you have found 'a good a thing' who is the wife. The favour that comes from marrying right are so many. This chapter discusses some of the opportunities which can come your way because you married right.

Spouses have become royals by reason of marriage

There are many people over the centuries who because of exceptional beauty or valour were selected to marry kings, queens, princes and princesses over the years past. People who had no royal blood but were subsequently given royal titles so they will fit into the royal house they had become part of. The story of the Hollywood actress Lisa Halaby who became queen Noor of Jordan after her marriage to King Hussein of Jordan is a typical example.

Overnight she was transformed from a popular Hollywood actress to a queen of a country and the first lady though she was not Jordanian. There are husband who have also benefited from marrying into royal houses and becoming royalty themselves because of marriage. Now that you are married to a royal, understand that you might have to support him or her when it comes to inheriting the throne of his or her ancestors in a God fearing way. Understand the responsibilities which may come your way because you are married to a royal or a traditional ruler and prepare your mind before it happens.

Spouses have become church leaders by reason of marriage

There are wives who marry founders of churches and son in laws who married the only daughter of a founder of a church who are then ushered into church leadership mostly because of their marriage. As I write this, my mind has been drawn to a powerful prayer camp in Ghana which is now a pale shadow of what it was when the founder was alive. Because her only daughter's husband became more influential when the founder died. This husband of her only daughter, who has now been ushered into church leadership by reason of marriage has now changed the very doctrine of the prayer camp and is now fallen out with the church the founder used to work with.

If you marry for only one reason love, you will be shocked to learn that the transitions within marriage may be so dramatic that your partner may not be prepared to handle it maturely. This young lady married a man she loved but he could not transitioned as a season minister of the word of God. This turn of events, has caused her to almost destroy the inheritance her mother left her. The once famous prayer camp is now a shadow of its former self. Understand dear reader that, within that beautiful woman you are marrying should also be a wife, co-pastor, business partner, mother and so on. A spouse, if he or she is the right one, will wear many hats to support his or her partner as the marriage progresses. One of the hats people are often reluctant to wear is the hat of a church leader or planter.

Now that you are married you should know that you are not going to partner your spouse in physical things only but also in leading the church of Christ where you find yourself.

Spouses have relocated abroad because of their marriages

All the pages of this book will not be enough to contain the many examples of spouses who had to relocate abroad because they married a spouse who stays or works there. I watched the documentary of an African young wife with a Chinese husband. This lady is from East Africa and had travelled all the way to China joined her husband in a small town in a less developed province. She was the only African every direction she looked and had to endure extreme loneliness when the husband was away working because she did not speak the language at the beginning. I also watched a YouTube video of another African lady who had joined her husband in faraway Iceland. A land she never in her wildest imagination dreamt of going to, let alone settle there to raise a family.

During the interview, she spoke of how different the culture is and the extremely cold weather she was having to endure after having stayed all her life in a very warm climate. Many husbands and wives especially, have had to go to literally the ends of the world to live with their spouses. A good spouse goes with you where you need him or her to be and makes your God his or her God and your people his or her people. Marriage gives the opportunity for spouses to join new families and even travel and live at places they never dreamt of going.

I watched a Mongolian wife who had followed her Nigerian husband to Nigerian and was seeking to return after the marriage had broken down beyond repair. Imagine that! I am 100% sure this Mongolian woman did not know much about Africa, let alone Nigeria before she met her husband. But the power of marriage had moved her from one remote part of the world to another to stay with her husband. A place, none of her descendants has had the opportunity to travel to. Marriage indeed takes you places you never thought of going.

Now that you are married ensure that where ever the marriage takes you works for your good as a child of God.

Spouses have inherited great fortunes by reason of their marriages

The reason some people are accused of being gold diggers is because in many marriages there is 'gold to dig 'by the less endowed partner. There will not be enough space in the pages of this book to talk about the many spouses whose families have been transformed for the better because of the wealth of their spouses. There are men and women whose marriages have brought great wealth and privilege to them. People have married into money or privilege, as is often said in developed countries.

There are families in Ghana where all the siblings and their children are now living abroad because their senior sister first went abroad through marriage. An opportunity they would not have had if their sister had not married a man who was living abroad. The horrors of marriages nowadays have masked the obvious advantages people get, because of who they married or the family they married into. So part of the reason marrying brings favour is because is connects you to the advantages or wealth of the family of your spouse. So marriage if done well does not only give you access to the love of your spouse but also the business connections and resources they have gathered over many years. No wonder some marriages are contracted to seal great business relationships between two rich families sometimes.

Now that you are married do not overlook the riches or wealth that your spouse's family has made available to you. Otherwise you would waste the opportunities it affords you.

Spouses have been ushered into leadership by reason of marriage

There are people who are first ladies of churches who never had the chance to even be class captains when they were growing up. People who have been ushered into leadership positions because of the man or woman they married. Anyone who marries a visionary will certainly have to be ready to be a vision bearer. There are ministries of international reach whose founders died suddenly and the lovely wives of the founder had to step up and lead these mega churches. There are at least two of such ministries I know in the country of Nigeria.

This does not only happen in Christian circles but also in politics. I know of at least two Members of Parliament (MP) who have been replaced by their wives after their death. Did I hear you say how? Yes it happened here in Ghana, and I will explain it to you: on those two occasions when the MP died suddenly there had to be a by election because the elections in Ghana are very competitive they had to choose someone the electorates were familiar with. Who best to replace the deceased than the wives who accompanied them everywhere they went as MPs. As I write to you these wives are discharging their duties as MPs creditably. They might not have planned to be MPs but because of the men they married they are now MPs in the parliament of Ghana.

This phenomenon does not only happened in churches or politics but can also happened in traditional leadership or kingship. From my reading of history, it even happened years ago, that spouses of emperors ended up becoming emperors themselves sometime especially after the sudden death of their spouse in the past in the empires of Russia and Ethiopia. Now that you are married, help push your husband or wife to the top because they will not go up there alone but certainly with you. If you are privileged to be married to a leader, do not just hide in his or her shadow but help them lead because you could be pushed into leadership on account of them in the near future.

Now that you are married understand that you are "one in everything" with your spouse, if they love to lead or it is their calling then you will have to learn from them because as they rise you would be required to rise with them or you will become a cog in their wheel instead of the helper you are meant to be.

PRAYER NUGGETS

You Will Have Opportunities You Never Had Before

1) Marriage has ushered people into leadership positions the never though they will occupy.
2) Marriage has given access to untold wealth of the husband or wife of some poor spouses.
3) Marriage has taken some spouses to countries they never planned to go to.

CHAPTER 12

YOUR TOGETHERNESS WILL INCREASE YOUR ABILITY TO DEAL WITH SOME THINGS

Ecclesiastes 4:9-12 King James Version

9 Two are better than one; because they have a good reward for their labour.10 For if they fall, the one will lift up his fellow: but woe to him that is alone when he falleth; for he hath not another to help him up.11 Again, if two lie together, then they have heat: but how can one be warm alone?12 And if one prevail against him, two shall withstand him; and a threefold cord is not quickly broken.

Because Of The Loving Support Of The Spouses

The above scripture is very clear on why being married will make you stronger in many situations. Marriage does not only deal with loneliness but it also helps the married man or woman deal with life issues i.e. life's cold shoulder, by keeping each other warm. Practically speaking tow people stand a better chance of dealing with cold weather if they band together but will succumbed to it if they stay away from each other. There many married people who would not have survived a very serious illness had it not been the encouragement and closeness of their spouses. There are even situations where people have managed to do a sports or train for a competition because their significant other was there to encourage them all the way.

Hence the saying, two are better than one. There are difficulties or challenges your relationships, training or even upbringing as a single person cannot deal with but your husband or wife might be the person with the contacts or strengths needed to deal with it. Mostly we marry people who compliment us in more ways than one. If we are introvert we often marry an extrovert; if we studied Arts we often marry those who studied pure sciences and if we are calculating we often end up with someone who is daring. Though can often be attributed to the phenomenon of 'opposite attracts' it is also because we seek for people who can do things that we are naturally not good at doing.

Because Couples Tend To Band Together

There are many situations where couples become extremely difficult to crack become they reinforce each other aspirations and believes. A typical example of how formidable a husband and wife team is the US gangster couple Bonnie and Clyde who became famous as formidable criminal gang. Because when a couple bring their minds together on an issue, it takes care of the male and female perspectives, the introvert and extrovert considerations, often the scientific or artistic flair for doing things and above all the believe in each other's strength or ideas. These strengths when they come together make them almost invincible: giving them abilities to deal with any issues life throws at them that they could not have withstood as unmarried individuals.

Married Couples Are A Three Fold Cord

The scripture above describes marriage as partnership between two people. Partnership where one comes to the aid of the other: a situation where one advantage compensate for the weakness of the other. A situation where one comes to the rescue of the other when they are in trouble. A couple is much more difficult to break because their combined physical and spiritual strengths together with the covering of God makes them a threefold cord. A couple who genuinely love each other and they together love God are unstoppable both in the physical and spiritual realms.

They are like a threefold cord which cannot be broken by any stress imposed upon it. They are like an impregnable fortress which cannot be broken into because of the many interwoven experiences, beliefs and desires they share together. Hence scripture admonishing Christians not to be unequally yoke with unbelievers because light and darkness cannot reinforce each other, rather one will weaken the other.

Your collective strength will make you more formidable

I am the more organised person between my wife and I but when it comes to routines involving spiritual practices she is better at it. For example when it comes to morning devotion once I am alerted to it most morning I will spring into action and if need be preach each morning of the year if I have to. But I will not remember to start most days if I am not prompted from time to time. My wife on the other hand loves to have the devotion take place every morning but due to other duties calling might not be available to partake in it. So we have me, being available for the devotion because I do not do much of the chores in the morning but not able to start it every morning whilst my wife will remember to start it every morning but might have to attend to other things during the devotion.

But our collective strength is for me to provide money to secure help with the chores so it will reduce the things she needs to do in the morning. I have also from my strength as the bread winner secured and assigned the task to an equally motivated young man who starts the devotion each morning so none of us will have to do it.

The strength of each spouse in a marriage ranges from their experiences, education, talents, careers, wealth, physique, beliefs, character and so one. Most of the time couples learn from the strengths of each other. An introvert will overtime become more extrovert if he or she is married to an extrovert and vice versa. Someone married to a highly educated person will tend to make more effort to study more to close the qualification gap.

An athletic husband will eventually whip up the interest of his wife in doing some form of exercises in the house. There are woman who can now teach or preach because their husbands who founded their churches kept encouraging them to do so. Every great ministry, business or organisation was either started or is still being managed by a husband and wife team. The collective strengths of a matured couple makes them a formidable team which can handle anything thrown at them.

Now that you are married be intentional about making the adage two heads are better than one true in your marriage. Be thankful to God for the new strengths and abilities you have acquired because of your marriage and work to make them even stronger.

PRAYER NUGGETS

Your Togetherness Will Increase Your Ability To Deal With Some Things

1) Your collective strength as a couple will make you more formidable than you were as individuals.
2) You will become are better team than any other team.
3) Your strength will cover each other's weakness and give you both the male and female perspective of everything.

CHAPTER 13

YOU WILL NOTICE THAT YOUR BEING MARRIED WILL MAKE DEALING WITH SOME SITUATIONS HARDER.

Deuteronomy 32:30 King James Version

30 How should one chase a thousand, and two put ten thousand to flight, except their Rock had sold them, and the Lord had shut them up?

The scripture above if not examined carefully will lead to the reader focusing only on the positive side of it. But there is a more disturbing part the scripture above that Christians often overlook. And it is the fact that 'a thousand can only be chased by one enemy and ten thousand two' because their rock has sold them or their Lord had shut them up. The same happens when a couple neglect their God or the needs of each other. Then what is supposed to be a formidable team makes you more vulnerable than when you were both single.

Difficulty With Undertaking Spiritual Exercises

There are many once vibrant young ladies and gentlemen who after marriage lose their drive for the things of God. This often happens because the spouse they married either does not take spiritual exercises seriously or he or she has not developed the discipline to keep the pace they had. Many once powerful single children of God are now a shadow of themselves because their spouses did not encourage or sometimes even opposed the things they did to keep themselves spiritually strong. I have seen several examples of women who found it difficult to come for church services because they married a backslider. Committed woman or men in the things of God who can no longer be seen regularly in church because of the difficulties or work, raising children or the burden of carrying a spouse who has lost their relationship with their maker. Now that you are married you will notice spiritual exercises like fasting and long waiting periods have become more difficult. Especially as the wife because your body does not belong to you alone but your husband.

Difficulty In Savings and Investments

Just like opposite attract when it comes to affection and bodily features in relationships, in the same way opposite also attract when it comes to attitude towards savings and investments. Most marriages have the saver and the spender. It is more difficult to make prudent financial decisions when the husband is the spender and the wife the saver. Spouses who have developed the discipline to leave within their means find it difficult to continue in that good habits once they marry a strong willed spender. This is especially hard when the spender is the husband or the breadwinner.

There are spouses who when they were not married used to be the one with money amongst their friends but are now always hard up because their spouses are not as careful with money as they are. Spouses who are addicted to buying the latest of everything they see. Spouses who buy things they cannot afford or spouses who buy on impulse. Now that you are married understand that the discipline you have concerning finances might not be shared by your spouse so make every effort to bring him or her to your level of understanding before it affects your future negatively.

There is a former English international footballer whose wife had to put limits on his credit card because he is addicted to buying exotic cars. Before this drastic measure by his wife he often returned home without warning with a new expensive car. No matter how rich you are, you cannot keep buying an expensive car every week without it having its toll on your finances and not to mention the space to keep them all.

Difficulty In Climbing The Corporate Ladder

Most desirable or top jobs include travelling at short notices to various places. When you are single you go anywhere you are sent without any issue with anyone. But the married has responsibilities to his or her family which cannot wait for anyone. Hence the marriages of most top CEOs, politicians and even founders of churches often falling apart. The married person will be spending most of these times away from the spouse. Many issues with spouses or children will require your attentions and so take you away from the work. The many responsibilities of family, if you want to be a good wife or husband will take some of the time you would have spent at work impressing your boss for one promotion or the other.

No wonder in many competitive job markets or in the developed world, marriages and especially the raising of a family seem to be out of the question for most young men and women who want to get to the top of major companies or corporations. What people forget is that there can be only few who ever make it to the boardroom. And in this world of uncertainties you are not even sure if your company will be around for the next five years. Is it worth it therefore to forgo having your family raised properly instead of fighting for a position which you might never get anyway? Now that you are married you need to decide which one takes priority your career or your family before you ruin both.

Difficulty In Helping The Needy

In African and in Ghana in particular, you do not marry an individual but a family. We often gloss over this saying till it comes back to bite us in the face. After marriage we suddenly realise that we have new needy people to pay attention to. Needy people from your side of the family and those from the other spouse's side of the family will team up to make demands on you. The people you believe were your family members suddenly more than double in most cases after marriage. Often before marriage, you choose when and who to help but after marriage your spouse will draw your attention to the fact that he or she is a relative and so cannot be ignored. This mostly happen in developing countries: people who did not bother you before you got married will start coming to ask for favours because they think only rich people have weddings.

Now that you are married you need to understand that your growing financial responsibilities if not managed well, would affect your ability to help the needy around you.

Difficulty In Remaining Attractive To Your Spouse

You and I know how if you are now married, how hard it was to keep our hands from each other as a dating couple. But you can now stay in the same room for days without the temptation to touch each other. Whilst this is not the case for a tiny few, it is almost universal for marriages which are five years and up. The question is, why it is so difficult to keep the attraction between the two of you before marriage, after marriage. Well it is because, most of us think getting a husband or wife requires effort but keeping one does not. Amusing as it might sound, most people do marriage on auto pilot but for courting and dating, with the attention of a jet fighter pilot. Hence the intense desires it generates.

Marriage has many unromantic duties: taking care of the house, children, bills, dealing with past hurts and so on. If care is not taken this mundane duties will be allowed to kill the romance which brought you together in the first place. It is more painful to lose a spouse than to lose a fiancé so by all means, intentionally do what your spouse find attractive from time to time to keep the flame of passion burning. There is nothing more unromantic than careless talk, bad dressing and smelling badly, please avoid these like the plague.

Now that you are married appreciate that you are the only one your spouse is allowed to desire sexually, so make every effort to make it worth their while.

You have done it before and can still do it in spite of the past fights, child birth, weight gain and the pending bills. These difficulties of life are easier to deal with when you know you are desired by the man or woman you love.

PRAYER NUGGETS

You Will Notice That You Being Together Will Make Dealing With Some Situations Harder.

1) You will notice that there are things which were easier for you before marriage but are know more difficult.
2) You will notice difficulty in remaining attractive to your spouse.
3) The difficulties of life are easier to deal with when you know you are desired by your wife or husband you love.

CHAPTER 14

YOU WILL NEED TO MODIFY YOUR OUTLOOK TOWARDS LIFE TO HAVE A SUCCESSFUL MARRIAGE

Introduction

Many people go into marriage expecting it to be either the same, different or better than what their parents had. In many cultures ladies are taught what to expect from the person they would marry and vice versa. In some cultures in Ghana the woman is told to let the man bear the burden of debt in the family alone but when it comes to him becoming worthy his wife is expected to bring that wealth home. Simply put 'the husband's debts is his own problems but his prosperity should be shared with the wife'. This an outlook towards marriage that has made many a married couple miserable and selfish. But this unchristian outlook or expectation of marriage is not only working against the husbands but also against the wives.

That same dominant culture of Ghana also teaches that a man's children belongs to the family of the woman and not the man. To put it bluntly, a man does not share the same family as his children. This understanding of marriage affected many children like me: fathers were reluctant to look after us because we were technically not his family members. If you were unlucky not to have an uncle or had an overburdened one, who had to take care of all the nephews and nieces of his sisters, then it meant 'game over' for you. My father's generations, were so conscious of this that whenever they got angry with your mom, it meant you, her children no longer got their fatherly care. After all doing it for you their daughter or son also meant they were doing it for your mom, whom they no longer liked.

Many fathers had to be taken to court, so they would be forced to look after their own children because culture had given them the idea that they were not relatives of theirs.

There are few difficulties which arise because people find themselves marrying under the matrilineal system of inheritance. But the reverse is also sometimes true for those marrying under the patrilineal system of inheritance. The outlook encourages the children to drift to the father's side of the marriage as against that of the mother. Because inheritance is done through the father the mother's side of the marriage often do not consider the children as their relatives. Hence such children hardly benefit from anything in the mothers family unless it is given the mother and she decides to pass it on to her children. However property belonging to the mother's family cannot be passed on to the woman's children in most cases.

But as born again Christians we can adopt a more healthy approach to marriage as we are led of the Holy Spirit. Many people go into marriage with different expectations, outlook and even temperament towards the spouse, only to change because of the nature of the marriage or the person they have married. There are marriages which have inspired the spouses to do and be, their best whilst others have brought out the worse in them. Under listed are scenarios which can change spouses after marriage.

Better Than Expected Marriages Can Change A Spouses Personality

We once visited a couple who were doing well in ministry: they were in charge in what was arguably the biggest prayer centre in Ghana. When we were ushered into their house we were all awed by the beauty and orderliness of the place. Then one elderly lady who had known the couple for years remarked. 'It appears the lessons on cleanliness and proper management of the house has finally been implemented by the pastor's wife.' She continued to explain, when we all turned in her direction with disbelief on our faces as to how a woman who is keeping a house that clean could once be so unkempt. Then she added this important point, which is the reason for this example, dirty Ama has really been transformed for the better by her marriage into 'clean Ama'. When she meant by that is that, Ama has been transformed into a better wife because her husband's rise in ministry inspired her to 'up her game' in cleaning the house' because the profile of people who came to visit kept increasing.

Again a lady friend of mine was looking at a picture of a lady she knew from childhood. She kept a examining the pictures so I became curious as asked her why, she then made a profound statement 'when you get a better than expected marriage it can even make you prettier than you were before marriage. Unfortunately the opposite also happen to pretty girls who find themselves in worse than expected marriages. Their beauty fades so rapidly that they become unrecognisable even to childhood friends. Now that you are married, you need to understand that a better marriage can change your personality for the better. A good marriage will enhance your good features and character traits.

Difficult Spouses Change The Disposition of Their Husbands Or Wives

Difficult spouses are those who refuse to work with you to solve the problems that come up during the marriage. People who refuse to act till challenges grow into major problems. There are perfectly confident women or men before marriage, who are now known to be jealous lovers because of the behaviour of their spouses. Partners who have refused to stop behaving inappropriately towards members of the opposite sex despite the protestation of their wife or husband. There are spouses whose husbands or wives unwillingness or inability to bring the needed income to the home has pushed them to develop a workaholic or even beggarly personality at work.

There are wives and even husbands who have become more daring or even flirtatious so they can find opportunities or resources for their children because of an unconcern or even an absentee husband's inability to discharge his duties creditably. There is an Akan proverb which says that 'if you see a frog hurrying alone then it means there two things are involved. Either it is chasing something or something is chasing it.' There are spouses who refuse to change jobs or go to school, so they can earn better incomes despite years of entreaties from their partners.

Difficult spouses who refuse to relocate from their current location, so they can be close to their family and others frustrating their spouses have contributed to making their concerned wives and husband's 'go getters' for the sake of the future of their children. Men and woman who were once laid back and content with what the lord had made.

Now that you are married pray that your husband or wife will be the man or woman respectively, you chose to marry and not a burden for you to carry.

Unforeseen Events In Marriage Can Changes Spouses Outlook Towards Life

I know of a once vibrant young man who is now quiet and withdrawn because and unforeseen event happened to him after marriage. All his children born to him turned out to be autistic: the kind that they cannot fend for themselves. People give birth to children to continue their legacy, but how can children who cannot even take care of themselves, take care of you the parent in your old age. The thoughts of who will take care of them when they, the parents are not around has killed the spirit of a once dynamic young man. Children who are so difficult to handle that when people visit refuse once they often do not go back after their first experience. A situation none of the spouses ever foresaw happening to them. This shock of an unplanned event has sucked the joy out of their once vibrant marriage.

The sudden loss of a child or children, collapsed of a once vibrant business and loss of employment of the breadwinner. I know of a couple whose marriage has been changed drastically because the husband lost his job ten years ago and has since never worked again till date. This has turned the wife to a hustler, who sells anything she can find to put food on the table of their still expanding family.

In my own case my family had to go through the unpleasant situation of secondary infertility for nine years before my wife finally took seed which led to a set of twin girls. During that unforeseen situation it affected both of us greatly. Because we thought everything will go well because we courted and married in purity. My ever smiling personality diminished. I sometimes when to church angry because I did not understand why those who disobeyed God before and even after seemed marriage to have as many children as they wanted whilst I could not even have one. I sometime asked the Lord in my prayers, how I would inspired these young ones in church to live holy lives as teens if my end is childlessness. Eventually my wife and I learnt to focus on serving the Lord even deeper in spite of our trials. He eventually honoured our sacrifices by giving as double for our trouble. Hallelujah!

Prayer Point

Now that you are married intercede for your family by telling the lord to not allow anything sudden happen to your family which will suck the joy out of your marriage. Together Pray against the plan of the enemy concerning your marriage.

PRAYER NUGGETS

You Will Need To Modify Your Temperament To Have A Successful Marriage

1) The attitude of your spouse in the marriage can force you to become a goal getter.
2) You might sometimes need to change you temperament or even career to cover the inabilities of your spouse.
3) A good marriage can transform a wife or husband into an even better spouse.

CHAPTER 15

YOUR MARRIAGE CAN TAKE YOU TO PLACES YOU NEVER PLANNED TO GO

Genesis 2:24 King James Version

24 Therefore shall a man leave his father and his mother, and shall cleave unto his wife: and they shall be one flesh.

Marriage Can Take You To Great Places

A prominent archbishop in Ghana was once sharing an opportunity he had to be at a great place because of his very well accomplished wife. And how he had to follow her lead in using the different types of cutlery sets which were placed before him for the different courses they ate that evening. Though he is a founder of a church and had travelled the world extensively for years. He had never had the opportunity by that time, to go to the White House in Washington D.C. The official residence of the American president. Despite his connections around the world, it took his marriage to a powerful African American activist to have access to the White House. Marriage is a lifelong partnership: as your spouse rises you rise with him or her. As they go places, you go with them. Pray you do not have to wish your spouse ill because he or she has chosen to go to great places without you.

It was the 50th anniversary of the republic of Ghana and it was streamed live around the world. The president of Ghana in a golden carriage with queen Elizabeth of Great Briton. But before then the president together with his wife had met the queen and her husband at the Buckingham palace as guests of the famous royal couple. The president's wife comes from a prominent political family in Ghana and had been to the United Kingdom a considerable number of time before this meeting.

But I believe without a shadow of doubt that never in her widest dream did she think she would one day be a guest in the Buckingham palace. But her marriage to the president of Ghana when the Nation attained the 50th anniversary of her independence gave her that rare opportunity. To see a West African first couple interact with the queen in her official residence was a source of great pride to all Africans around the world.

Now that you are married: Keep pushing each other as a couple to greater heights whenever the opportunity arises. You may never know where it will take you both.

Marriage Can Take You To Difficult Places

Marriage can take you to difficult places you never taught you would be. I watched a movie where an American white woman married an Iranian man. The man was very loving and caring. After they had a son, the husband suggested that they went home to visit his parents because he had not seen them for over a decade. This is a true story that had been adapted into a film. It was during the height of the Iranian revolutions so Americans or whites were not welcome there so for the woman to cross the border with her husband she had to be put in the boot in that hot arid region.

A woman raised in suburban America who was used to all the comforts of a middle class life at the time. But because of who she had married she found herself hiding in the boot of a car for hours. Eventually she arrived at the husband hometown. Immediately they got there he took her passport and destroyed it and became a typical abusive husband. Her marriage had taken her to a difficult region where a woman is considered as half the value of a man. Her marriage had taken her to a place which still lived by the principals of a 7th century Arabia prophet.

An African woman married a Chinese man and moved to one of the remote areas in China to be with his family. The man could not get a Chinese woman to marry because the China's One Child Policy had resulted in more than 30 million men of marriageable age without women to marry. She was the only African in the small town and did not speak mandarin at the time. She could not interact with her new family due to the language barrier. And her husband worked long hours outside the home. She had married into great loneliness and had no one to turn to. Her desire to marry and leave her poverty stricken town in Uganda had taken her to a place of loneliness and isolation in the Far East.

The two extreme examples above concern wives who married into difficult places. But had to strengthen themselves to overcome the difficulties they found themselves. The American wife eventually strengthen herself and hatched a plan to escape from her husband back to America without her child. The Ugandan woman however decided to integrate into the society s and learnt to speak mandarin quickly.

She eventually started communicating with her in-laws who became fond of her. She subsequently opened an account on Weibo, the Chinese version of YouTube, where she shares her experiences with tens of thousands of people in China. Though she was once a lonely wife, she is now a celebrity in her own right in China. She had with much effort made something good out of her difficult situation. Because he Weibo account also gives her some income to support herself on those back at home.

Marriage Can Take You To Strange Places

I was once watching a documentary on conjugal rights in some prisons in the United States of America. I watched in shock as they explained how some married people whose spouses were outside the prisons had fought for conjugal rights with their partners.

I do not think any of them in their wildest imagination saw themselves fulfilling their marriage bed duties in a prison of all places. In a strange environment full of all kinds of criminals.

Before you think such a situation is far from you let me tell you how easy it is to end up in prison. Your spouse could end up in prison because of a well-orchestrated frame up. Your spouse could end up in prison because a government he or she was part of had been overthrown in a coup. Your spouse could be in prison pending the outcome of a case he or she might even be innocent of. And above all your spouse could be in prisoned for preaching the gospel or even carrying in certain places or countries a bible.

Now that you are married, you need to understand that where your spouse is or finds himself or herself is where you are supposed to be. Thus, it is better to be with your spouse at strange places to keep the marriage bond, than to wait to be close to him at more familiar places. That 'wait for better circumstance' approach to marriage has left many spouses separated from each other for years at a time.

Marriage Can Take You To Evil Places

There are people who were raised as Christians and never went anywhere evil. People, who all their lives were raised to fear God and His word. But the difficulties of marriages finally drove them to the occult or a fetish priest. I do not know where you are reading this from. But here in Africa, not having a child is a very big deal indeed. Some Christian mothers have been known to, out of frustration, even encouraged their sons to take a second wife or divorce the first one.

The incessant pressure of close relatives on married couples to give birth has driven a number of them to seek unconventional means to get them. Some now go as far as using surrogate mothers to birth the very expensive babies. To ease the pressure on them.

Some wives have ended up in prison because they faked their kidnapping to cover a false pregnancy they had been using to extort money from their partners. Others ended up in the shrines of fetishes and scammers despite their Christian upbringing, all in a bid to give birth to secure their fragile marriages. Marriages if mismanaged can take us to the darkest of places.

Indeed there are people on death roll out now in many prisons around the world because of bad marriages. People who have killed their spouses for one reason or the other. People who have killed their spouses out of anger and those who killed them in cold blood after years of planning and scheming. Marriage if you allow it can change you for the worst instead of for the better. Others killed them to hide a secret or to keep property they have made together to themselves. Still others have been sentenced to life permanently or for the rest of their lives because of what they did to their spouses out of spite, suspicion or anger.

Now that you are married, you need to understand that it takes people who are close to each other to hurt each other. The Akan people of Ghana have an adage which says 'it is two trees closed to each other that will from to time scratch each other'. People who are far from you and do not interact with you cannot hurt you. The belief that your love one can never hurt you is false and frankly childish. Attempts should rather be made by each spouse to minimise the number of time they intentionally hurt one other.

PRAYER NUGGETS

Your Marriage Will Take You To Places You Never Planned To Go
1) Pray that your marriage does not take you to evil places and people.
2) Pray for strength to deal with the strange places your marriage might take you to.
3) Pray that your marriage will take you to great places in life as you rise in your careers and ministries.

CHAPTER 16

YOU WILL SAY NO TO THINGS YOU NEVER THOUGHT YOU COULD

1 Corinthians 7:33-34 King James Version

33 But he that is married careth for the things that are of the world, how he may please his wife. 34 There is difference also between a wife and a virgin. The unmarried woman careth for the things of the Lord, that she may be holy both in body and in spirit: but she that is married careth for the things of the world, how she may please her husband.

Marriage Changes People

It is true that marriage changes people: one of the ways that change manifest is the things you will say no to after marriage. No matter how righteous you were before marriage, there will be things you used to do that you will say no to after marriage. And there are many good reasons for that: most of the no's you will say will help make room for you to spend time with your spouse. Others will be because you do not want to offend your partner. Still others will be because you do not want to unnecessary stir jealousy in your partner. Saying no to a past life or way of doing things has a way of making a new spouse feel special and catered for.

I am Going Home To My Wife

I remember years ago a colleague of mine who was known to be a serious womanizer before he married his wife rushing home during break to eat lunch at home with his new wife. His friends thought his commitment to the new marriage was too much and wondered how long it would last. But they soon realised that his many no's to their requests for him to join them at places they used to frequent was dragging on year after year. He had been changed by the virtuous woman he married and as I speak has learnt to say no to late night outs and the wanton womanizing he was known for.

You Will Say No To Mom and Dad's Largesse

Let us take a hypothetical case of a privileged young woman who is accustomed to not having to take care of anyone. The freedom to eat out anytime she went out with family, friends or even loved ones. They joy of having very little responsibility around the house. Very little household chores available to keep her occupied as a student or young worker. As a young adult she still has access to mom and dad for all the things she will ever need. The chance to partake in their already established lives and the luxuries it provides. The chance to travel abroad or even further her post graduate course outside the country if she so chose to. But one day she finds the man of her dreams and everything changes. Every plan the parents had for receives an emphatic no, if it contradicts her plans with her husband. She shelves or says not to the plan to do her post graduate and rather embraces the new responsibility of being a wife and mother. Though hypothetical in this scenario, this situation is playing out in many affluent homes around the world.

She now finds being alone boring and desires to see her husband all the time. This new wife then says no to staying in her father's mansion but rather choses to go and stay in her husband small flat instead. She stops driving her father's cars and chooses to share a taxi with her husband. If she had a car, she says not to drive it herself and hands the keys to her husband to rather drive it. Because she feels better being driven around by her husband than driving herself. Indeed marriage will make you say no to things you never thought you could.

You Will Say No To Staying Alone

Most of us, especially the men loved our freedom as young men staying alone. We ate when we wanted and went in and out at any time we pleased. There was no one around to instruct us on where to put what or on what to eat. We bought what we wanted and arranged things in our rooms the way we found to be convenient. Then we marry and bring someone's daughter into our house because we no longer want to be alone. This young lady then takes over our lives and begins slowly but surely to say no to all we ever did to our own apartment, to suit her 'high standards'. Suddenly we are no longer interested in going anywhere alone and certainly stopped desiring to come home to meet the house empty again. We begin to say no to, sleeping alone in our own beds and begin to detest cooking for ourselves or even buying food to eat from vendors on a regular basis.

You Will Say No To Great Opportunities

Marriage is a calling like the other callings we are so familiar with like ministry because it requires your entire being to make it work well. Marriage is a calling because it will occupy you for life. It is an endeavour only death will relief you of: your death or the death of your spouse. Where am I going with this? If a calling requires sacrifices, so does marriage. However the sacrifices people make in marriages are often described as blind love or plain foolishness. That could not be further from the truth because marriage by nature requires the couple to say no, to many desirable things to make them work.

A marriage only works when the couple say no to what appears to be lucrative opportunities on the surface. Marriage couples say no to opportunities which was once desired before marriage but has now been brought back on a silver platter. Marriage couples say no to fantastic opportunities which will keep them from being with their spouse most of the time. I know of spouses who have turned down the opportunity to leave abroad because their spouse is here in Ghana. Still other spouses turn down great careers or opportunities far away in order to stay in the same house with their spouses.

Married people who have not followed this principal have sometimes ended up with great careers but suffered broken homes. Because their attention was focused on the job to the neglect of their families. The saddest thing with dedicating your life to something which does not belong to you is that, you may end up losing it all together eventually. Some have eventually lost the careers they dedicated their lives to in addition to producing wayward children and broken marriages.

Now that you are married, understand that there are things or people you might have loved so much in the past (i.e. before you got married) that you have to deny yourself of now for the protection of your marriage.

PRAYER NUGGETS

You Will Say No To Things You Never Thought You Could

1) I pray that you will say no to great opportunities which will lead to a broken home or wayward children.
2) I pray that a time comes when you will say no to living with your parents and strike out on your own.
3) I pray a time will come when you will say no to living alone as a single person because you found a life partner.

CHAPTER 17

YOU WILL SAY YES TO THINGS YOU NEVER THOUGHT YOU COULD

Genesis 3:6 New International Version

6 When the woman saw that the fruit of the tree was good for food and pleasing to the eye, and also desirable for gaining wisdom, she took some and ate it. She also gave some to her husband, who was with her, and he ate it.

Before I got married I used to wonder why Adam was not man enough, to say no to the eating of the fruit in the Garden of Eden, when his wife Eve offered it to him. Such questions easily flow from the lips of single men and women because they have no idea the things you will say yes to in a marriage relationship. When you are married to someone you love, you usually and as far as it is within your power, want to do things which will make your spouse happy with herself or himself and obviously with you. There are wives who said yes to their husbands request for them to go into prostitution so they can survive in a hostile country they had travelled to. Something she would never have even thought of doing if she was not married.

We see Abraham and Isaac convincing their wives to say they are their brothers so they can save their lives. Essentially what Abraham and Isaac asked of their wives was to ignore the fact that they are married and rather say they are their brothers so they could marry other men. It also means that Abraham and Isaac Instead of fighting for their wives decided to sell them to the highest bidder for their safety and wealth.

If you think I am exaggerating then come with me as we read the book of Genesis chapter 12

Genesis 12:10-17 King James Version

[10] And there was a famine in the land: and Abram went down into Egypt to sojourn there; for the famine was grievous in the land. [11] And it came to pass, when he was come near to enter into Egypt, that he said unto Sarai his wife, Behold now, I know that thou art a fair woman to look upon: [12] Therefore it shall come to pass, when the Egyptians shall see thee, that they shall say, This is his wife: and they will kill me, but they will save thee alive. [13] Say, I pray thee, thou art my sister: that it may be well with me for thy sake; and my soul shall live because of thee.

[14] And it came to pass, that, when Abram was come into Egypt, the Egyptians beheld the woman that she was very fair. [15] The princes also of Pharaoh saw her, and commended her before Pharaoh: and the woman was taken into Pharaoh's house. [16] And he entreated Abram well for her sake: and he had sheep, and oxen, and he asses, and menservants, and maidservants, and she asses, and camels. [17] And the Lord plagued Pharaoh and his house with great plagues because of Sarai Abram's wife.

From the passage above we can see that Abraham was not super human as Christians often assume. He sold out his own wife and comfortable pocketed the proceeds till Jehovah himself intervened. The passage above say 'Abraham was treated well because of his wife Sarah. Imagine that: he was content with surviving so another man could take his wife, king or not.

He did not do it in Egypt alone but also in Gerar in the land of Canaan before Abimelech the King. So for the second time Sarah had to say yes to 'pretending to be his sister' to protect him.

Genesis 20:1 King James Version

20 And Abraham journeyed from thence toward the south country, and dwelled between Kadesh and Shur, and sojourned in Gerar.² And Abraham said of Sarah his wife, She is my sister: and Abimelech king of Gerar sent, and took Sarah.³ But God came to Abimelech in a dream by night, and said to him, Behold, thou art but a dead man, for the woman which thou hast taken; for she is a man's wife.⁴ But Abimelech had not come near her: and he said, Lord, wilt thou slay also a righteous nation?⁵ Said he not unto me, She is my sister? and she, even she herself said, He is my brother: in the integrity of my heart and innocency of my hands have I done this.

I can imagine all the lies she had to say yes to, so as to fulfil the request of her husband to protect him. If the father of faith could do this in a dangerous and difficult land, then I am sure you are no longer surprised people ask their wives to sell their bodies for money in foreign lands when things are difficult. Truly the apple does not fall far from the tree. Isaac who was not born by the above episode between his mother and father also asked the wife to do a similar thing. Let us look into that too:

Genesis 26:6-9 King James Version

⁶ And Isaac dwelt in Gerar:⁷ And the men of the place asked him of his wife; and he said, She is my sister: for he feared to say, She is my wife; lest, said he, the men of the place should kill me for Rebekah; because she was fair to look upon.⁸ And it came to pass, when he had been there a long time, that Abimelech king of the Philistines looked out at a window, and saw, and, behold, Isaac was sporting with Rebekah his wife.⁹ And Abimelech called Isaac, and said, Behold, of a surety she is thy wife; and how saidst thou, She is my sister? And Isaac said unto him, Because I said, Lest I die for her.

So in the passage above we see Isaac also convincing the wife to pretend to be his sister to protect him from harm. I do not know whom he learnt this behavior from? Whether from the father Abraham or mother Sarah or he caught it by inspiration.

Now that you are married you will say yes to many difficult life choices to help advance the course of your family. Examples could be:

1) Relocating to a difficult area to live together with your spouse.
2) Picking a less lucrative career so you can raise your children.
3) Taking time off work to be a homemaker.
4) Becoming the mother of a young ministry.
5) Living far below the life you are used to so as to help your spouse.

Now that you are married note that there will be certain unholy requests from your spouse or relatives that you should never say yes to. Examples could be:

1) A request to sell your body for money.
2) A request to commit a crime for their benefit.
3) A request to deny that you are his wife or her husband.
4) A request to use your naked pictures or video to scam others for their money.

If Mr. Adam had said no to Mrs Adam's request for him to eat the forbidden fruit, she would have sinned alone and would have been replaced with Eve 2.0 And the sinner Eve 1.0 kicked out of the garden so humanity would have been spared of the problem of the original sin which runs through our blood from generation to generation.

PRAYER NUGGETS

You Will Say Yes To Things You Never Though You Could

1) I pray that you will say not to unholy request from your spouse or relatives.
2) I pray you say yes to living within your husband's budget even if you are accustomed to something higher
3) I pray you say yes to whatever it takes for you and your spouse to rise in life

CHAPTER 18

YOU WILL LEARN TO CHANGE YOUR VIEWS ON MANY THINGS IN YOUR LIFE

Introduction

Exodus 32:13-14 Amplified Bible

13 Remember Abraham, Isaac, and Israel (Jacob), Your servants to whom You swore [an oath] by Yourself, and said to them, 'I will multiply your descendants as the stars of the heavens, and all this land of which I have spoken I will give to your descendants, and they shall inherit it forever.'" 14 So the Lord changed His mind about the harm which He had said He would do to His people.

In my book entitled *20 things I wish I had mastered by age 30 for a life of excellence* I made a profound statement. That divorce and breaks in relationships are often cause by bad habits of one or both of the partners. That people often break relationships because they are not able to cope with the bad habit of an unrepentant spouse or fiancé. So for people's marriages to work they often have to undo certain habits they have and redo or pick up certain good habits they might have left by the wayside of the typical 'you do me I do you' life of the ordinary person.

People who never change their minds are some of the most difficult people to live with. Because they live as though they can never make a mistake. Such people are often very critical of others but are sure in their own minds that they can never do wrong. Spouses with this attitude are proud and have little regard for the man or woman they have married. They are often puffed up by some exposure they have had in terms of education or experience. A man or woman who cannot change his mind or his ways ever, is dead to counsel no matter how sound it may be and is set in his or her ways forever.

As we mature in life we learn from others. We also learn by evaluating the consequences of our past actions. We often realise that things we might have imbibed as gospel truths may not be so. We also observe the life of others in similar circumstances such as ours and adjust our ways so we do not end up like them. Thus using other people's experiences or lessons to shape our own lives. Nothing in life is set in stone: you only keep a certain outlook in life because it helps take care of your mental and physiological health. In Christianity there is the word of God which is our guide as Christians and then for our daily directions we have the Holy Spirit and our sanctified consciences as believers.

You Will Change Your Views On Discipline

Proverbs 23:13-14 King James Version

[13] Withhold not correction from the child: for if thou beatest him with the rod, he shall not die. [14] Thou shalt beat him with the rod, and shalt deliver his soul from hell.

The tussle between daddy and mommy on how to discipline children can become a big issue. I know wives who so interfered with their husband mode of discipline and out of frustration the husband decided not to discipline the children ever again. Imagine the disaster that would result if this aggrieved husband does not change his mind in time to prevent his children from going out of hand. But as the children grow it will be the mother who will call for more discipline because her earlier protestation was based more on the fact that the children will be hurt than the fact that they needed not to be discipline.

So in a marriage the one who used to shield the children from the rod will eventually be calling for it when he or she begins seeing their entreaties being ignored by children who have no fear of consequence. Then the father or mother who was initially very enthusiastic in 'not sparing the rod' will with time observe the children becoming more and more are afraid of him or her instead of loving and respecting him or her respectively. Depending on how a child or children respond to the discipline of the parents, thy may either intensify their mode of correction or lessen it. Again the father with time, tend to be stricter on the boys whilst the mother does the same with the girls. This become worst when they start showing some of the wayward behaviours the parents exhibited in their own teens.

Now that you are married remember not to fight your husband or wife over his or her views on how children should be disciplined because few years down the line you might wish he or she had even been stricter. Learn to always back each other when it comes to discipline and discus any excesses in your closet as a couple. Never let your children feel you side with them against the one disciplining them or they will see it as an act of aggression instead of something to straighten them up.

You Will Change Your Views On Education

Ecclesiastes 12:11-13 21st Century King James Version

[11] The words of the wise are as goads, and as nails fastened by the master builders, which are given from one Shepherd. [12] And further, my son, by these words be admonished: of making many books there is no end, and much study is a weariness to the flesh. [13] Let us hear the conclusion of the whole matter: Fear God and keep His commandments, for this is the whole duty of man.

There are people who have strange views when it comes to education. These strange ideas when brought into a marriage can cause many problems. But education is so important that, the scripture above describes it as the nails or fasteners which we use to fasten the pieces of our lives together. As a couple your marriage will be 'all over the place' unless it is bound together with knowledge from relevant education. There is not a single dollar millionaire or person doing well on the world stage who is not a continuous learner or into self-learning.

There are people who have been brought up with the view that, there is such a thing as 'too much education'. That doing advanced degrees, though they qualify for it, will make them worldly. No one who is using the knowledge he or she is acquiring to help humanity can be said to have had too education. Over educated people, if there is even such a thing, are people who are piling up degrees upon degrees without using them to fulfil any purpose.

You Will Change Your Views On Money

Ecclesiastes 7:12 King James Version

12 For wisdom is a defence, and money is a defence: but the excellency of knowledge is, that wisdom giveth life to them that have it.

There are many funny ideas that singles have about money. Ideas learnt from home or picked from people in the neighbourhood where they grew up. Ideas like 'I this family we are poor but proud' so be careful of your aspirations because and again you know that 'money does not grow on trees' so keep your expectation down. What are you asking me to pay for 'do you think I print money?' Our ancestor also say 'we do not search for riches but we rather get it when the circumstances are right' Again people advise us not strive to be rich because we 'came into this world with nothing and we will certainly take nothing out when we die'.

Depending on how we understand the above quotes we model our life to reflect it. There are woman who before marriage thought they needed to make money to take care of only themselves because the husband in the future will take care of the rest. Then there are others who believe their only job is to look beautiful and healthy because husband to be will take care of every other need of the family.

Then there are men who think 'so long as a woman is God fearing and loves me, money will not be an issue in our marriage.' Still some men think because 'I am marrying a graduate she will hold her half of the financial responsibilities in the marriage.

All or at least most of the above views on marriage, will have to change for the marriage to grow stronger. As the marriage progresses you will notice how many issues will quickly lead to conflict. Simple disagreement will degenerate into serious conflict because they solutions 'money' is not available. A simple sickness of a child can lead to a life threatening situation because money was not there to send him or her to a good hospital early. Whether you thought money was important or not you will soon realise how many problem it solves in your house. Those who thought taking about money was a sign of carnality will soon find themselves thinking about it every day of their life because they need it for day to day management of the home.

For the husband's peace of mind to remain, the wife will expect him to provide the basic things in life. Basic necessities which run out every month or so and have to be replenished. Expenses which crop up every semester or term. Birthday which pop up once a year and many other anniversaries which require celebrations or outings. It is then that your view on money will change to reflect what the scripture above is saying. Money does not only answer most things in marriage but it also acts as a defence against the financial problems which threaten to destroy it. As the years go by and the cost of everything around you increases far above the rates of increase of your salaries, you will change your mind on whether savings or investing today for a better tomorrow is a sound advice.

Now that you are married, you will soon discover that money as a tool, if properly used will save you a lot of stress. Now that you are married you will soon realise, it is not prudent to spend most of your time as a spouse looking for money. However, it is equally bad to never make the money your family needs to take care of their expenses. Now that you are married you will soon realise you can eliminate 70% of the problems which lead to divorce by becoming financially independent. And by working hard enough to secure the necessary finances to carter for the many needs which arise from time to time in a home.

PRAYER NUGGETS

You Will Learn To Change Your Views On Many Things In Your Life

1) I pray money or the lack of it does not destroy your marriage.
2) I pray your mind set about money changes in time to make you a great spouse.
3) I pray you change the things which need changing and relearn those which need relearning to improve upon the way you marry.

CHAPTER 19

YOUR MOTIVATION FOR DOING THINGS WILL MOSTLY BE MEMBERS OF YOUR FAMILY INSTEAD OF YOUR PERSONAL NEEDS

Genesis 27:12-13 King James Version

12 My father peradventure will feel me, and I shall seem to him as a deceiver; and I shall bring a curse upon me, and not a blessing. 13 And his mother said unto him, Upon me be thy curse, my son: only obey my voice, and go fetch me them.

Introduction

The above story talks about Mrs Rebekah Isaac telling the youngest twin out of his two sons to steal the blessings from his senior brother Esau. But Rebekah from the very time they struggled in her womb had received a word of prophesy that the senior will serve the younger. Then she watched in horror as her eldest son sold his seniority to his junior brother for a pot of soup. She then determined to never allow the family's blessing to pass onto the wrong son. As a result, she purposed to rather ensure that the junior son, who she believed was more deserving got the blessing instead of her irresponsible senior son. She planned to ensure Jacob got the blessings irrespective of whatever consequences arose, if it was later discovered that she tricked her husband.

In the verses above, we see a wife and a mother overriding her love for her husband to ensure the prophetic word she received before her children were born came to pass. She then declared to her son that, she will bear the curse from the son deceiving a man of God, for the blessing on the family to pass to the right son.

Many Are Moved By The Motivation For Their Children To Do Better Than Them

There are wives who have become combatant and contentious because they are motivated by the desire to push their children beyond where they reached in education and hence life. Wives who go as far as fighting with their one time darling husbands to ensure they send their children to the right standard of school, which according to them, will ensure their academic success. Parents sometime forgo very important things in their own lives to ensure the children are in a good private school.

Even the wives who find themselves in situations where the husband is not financial sound who usually abandon dressing up to be attractive to them and rather plunge themselves in all kinds enterprises to find the finances to push the children to the best of schools. Most of the time when you see mothers in this situation, it is as though they have never been fashionistas before, you may be convinced she was not the one whose dressing used to drive her husband crazy in the past.

But she mostly forgoes that power of looking attractive so she can concentrate on satisfying the desires for her children, who often need her attentions constantly. This desire to serve the children with her skills and strengths can lead to a situation where her own personality and aspirations are forgotten.

There are many parents or couples who are identified by their children's names. You may often hear references like 'Rachel's mother or Fred's father' because the couple's concentration is on their children instead of themselves. Some couples overdo this, forgetting that they need to thrive as parents for them to be in a position to help push the children far beyond where they reached in life.

Some husbands also reduce their clothing to very few, refusing to buy new ones, so they can invest in the children's future.

Many Married People are Moved By The Motivation To Make Their Spouses Happy

Many spouses' motivation for doing many things in their marriage is for the happiness of their husbands or wives. There are husbands for instance, who have lived with their mother in laws for years in their matrimonial home, forgoing their privacy in the process, so their wives will be happy. There are spouses who have raised siblings, nephews, nieces and even children of wives or husbands to make them happy.

There are husbands who work very hard but never use the proceeds on themselves. There are Husbands who go about looking destitute because they are paying fees which takes almost all their earnings. There are even parents who have reduced the number of times they eat so they can save enough to provide for housekeeping money for their homes. The average couple are often motivated by something besides each other's self-interest: How to push their families forward. And the motivation to help others sometimes extend beyond the nuclear family of the spouse. There are spouses who have gone out of their ways to help the siblings or even cousins of their spouses. Usually this is considered as a Labour of love to make their spouses happy.

Now that you are married you need to realise that the meaning of 'the two shall become one flesh' also encompasses your desire to do for him or her what he or she cannot do for himself or herself respectively. You as a young wife or husband will be moved often by concern for the future, fear of averting the things which can go wrong and sometimes premonition to act on behalf of your spouse or children.

PRAYER NUGGETS

Your Motivation For Doing Things Will Mostly Be Members Of Your Family Instead Of Your Personal Needs

1) I pray couples will do all it takes to ensure their children achieve greater things then them.
2) I pray the struggle of wives to see the welfare of their children or child will not affect their marriages wrongly.
3) I pray the motivation to make a spouse happy will not leave the other spouse unhappy in the marriage.

CHAPTER 20

YOU WILL BECOME AWARE OF THE OVERWHELMING NEED TO PRAY ABOUT YOUR FAMILY

Philippians 4:6-8 King James Version

6 Be careful for nothing; but in everything by prayer and supplication with thanksgiving let your requests be made known unto God.7 And the peace of God, which passeth all understanding, shall keep your hearts and minds through Christ Jesus.

Most time when we are young we believe we are invincible. You will hear many young pastors talk about how they cannot fall sick or will never take medicine by faith because they believe in divine health. But when those same preachers reach their sixties, you see them begin to move slower on the platform than they used to. Others begin to wear glasses whilst reading as if it is not a medical intervention.

Then you begin to hear others talk about trips abroad for medical check-ups. And a recommendation for the congregation to take seriously the message of living a healthy lifestyle in their messages. The bold declaration of them seeing at 80 years like Caleb who could see at 80 the way he saw at 40 gradually disappear. Because the reality of the body being weak begins to dawn on them. Our lord Jesus boldly alluded to the medical difficulties of old age when he said to Peter: you will be led to places you do not want to go in your old age. He used this 'young to old man' analogy to illustrate that, when Peter is old in his ministry he will be led by the enemies of the gospel to places he would otherwise not go as a young energetic preacher.

John 21:18 King James Version

18 Verily, verily, I say unto thee, When thou wast young, thou girdest thyself, and walkedst whither thou wouldest: but when thou shalt be old, thou shalt stretch forth thy hands, and another shall gird thee, and carry thee whither thou wouldest not.

In the same way marriage is considered to be part of the maturing processes in life within all cultures. That is why in every ancient civilisation till date, a boy and a girl needs to first go though the right of passage into adulthoods before marriage. Many of the things you used to gloss over will suddenly become 'a life and death situation when you marry'. Difficulties with relationships before marriage which seemed insignificant, will suddenly become more intense because of the permanent nature of the marriage relationship. People who were not related to you but belonged to your spouse's family will suddenly become your in laws.

Again by reason of your marriage, the witches in your family gain the legal right to collaborate with the ones in your spouse's family to fight against your union and the plans which go with it. And many other difficulties which might arise in a marriage as explained in the previous chapters will all necessitate that you pray as married person more than you did even as single individual persons. Unfortunately the opposite is the situation for most married people who think marriage is an environment to relax from intensive intercessory prayers.

Many Issues Within The Marriage Will Call For Prayers

Prayer for children both born and unborn

Exodus 23:26 Amplified Bible

26 No one shall suffer miscarriage or be barren in your land; I will fulfill the number of your days.

You become aware of the need to pray about your children before they are born. Praying they will be healthy and obedient to your instructions. Praying the two of you will have the anointing to bear them in time and without incident. Praying your children will be brilliant and make the right choices as they grow up. Praying that the people who come to stay with you will not be a bad influence on your children and so on.

Prayer About Work And Income Generation.

Exodus 23:25 Amplified Bible

25 You shall serve [only] the Lord your God, and He shall bless your bread and water. I will also remove sickness from among you

Pray your ability to earn an income to cater for the family will improve with increasing expenses. Pray that your work becomes something you have gifts, talents or skills for and love doing. You will need to pray your work will not keep your family apart for far too long to lead to temptation to the both of you. Pray that your work will make way for you to have a great relationship with your children. Pray that your work will not take all your time to a point where it interfere with your worship with your God.

Prayer For Your In-laws

Pray that your relationship with your in-laws will be great. Pray your in-laws will be allies and not adversaries. Pray that your in-laws will not influence your spouse negatively. Pray your in-laws become an assert and not a liability to your marriage.

Matthew 10:35-37 Amplified Bible

35 For I have come to set a man against his father, and a daughter against her mother, and a daughter-in-law against her mother-in-law; 36 and a man's enemies will be the members of his [own] household [when one believes and another does not].

Pray About Your Plans For The Future

Pray about the plans you have as a family because we can prepare the horse for battle but it is the lord who gives victory. Again many are the plans of men but only the counsel of the lord will stand. Pray that as a family your plan agree with the purposes of God for your lives.

Proverbs 19:20-22 Amplified Bible

20 Listen to counsel, receive instruction, and accept correction, That you may be wise in the time to come. 21 Many plans are in a man's mind, But it is the Lord's purpose for him that will stand (be carried out).

Pray For Long life and Health

Psalm 91:16 King James Version

16 With long life will I satisfy him, and shew him my salvation.

You have every right as a child of God to pray for long life and health. Remember health is not that you never fall sick but that when you fall sick you recover quickly. Meaning, you are healthy most of the time and the occasional times you are sick you recover whether through medicine or divine intervention as a family till you live out all your years on earth. Heaven is for eternity you should not be in a rush to go there and leave your young family behind to fend for themselves. Pray you will live to see all your grandchildren, if Jesus tarries.

How To Pray For The Family

Plead the blood

Hebrews 9:22 King James Version

22 And almost all things are by the law purged with blood; and without shedding of blood is no remission.

Plead the blood that was shed on Calvary as you intercede for them in whatever sin the find themselves in. No matter what you feel at the time still pray that the Lord will look on the blood of His son and forgive and reform them back to a relationship with him. Pray no family member will be lost to the devil in any way shape or form.

Mark with the blood

Exodus 12:13 Amplified Bible

13 The blood shall be a sign for you on [the doorposts of] the houses where you live; when I see the blood I shall pass over you, and no affliction shall happen to you to destroy you when I strike the land of Egypt.

Mark every child, property, food and location you reside with the blood of Jesus. Pray like the Israelites in Egypt the lord will spare your family from any pandemic or disaster whether natural or man-made. Mark your family vehicle with the blood of Jesus against accidents and theft. Mark your food against accidental and intentional poison. Mark your food against natural and spiritual poisons. Mark you family against affliction by occultist and diviners who go around afflicting people with chronic sicknesses. Do these prayers whenever the Holy Spirit prompts you to do so without delay.

Issue Decrees On Your Family's Behalf

Job 22:26-29   King James Version

²⁶ For then shalt thou have thy delight in the Almighty, and shalt lift up thy face unto God.²⁷ Thou shalt make thy prayer unto him, and he shall hear thee, and thou shalt pay thy vows.²⁸ Thou shalt also decree a thing, and it shall be established unto thee: and the light shall shine upon thy ways.²⁹ When men are cast down, then thou shalt say, There is lifting up; and he shall save the humble person.

As you serve the lord in sincerity and give him of your substance as a family it places you in a position to make decrees on its behalf.

Decrees that bad things happening in the family will change for the better. Say from your heart:

'When men are cast down, then thou shalt say, There is lifting up'

The good things you want to happen in your family you will decree them into existence

'Thou shalt also decree a thing, and it shall be established unto thee'

Decree that hidden gems in terms of talent, gifts and skills in your family shall be revealed. Say from your hear: *'and the light shall shine upon thy ways'*

Decree that at all materials time every family member will choose humility before God instead of the pride of life which begins all rebellion in the flesh and spirit.

MY PRAYER FOR YOU

I Pray Your Family Turns Out To Be All That You Have Ever Prayed Them To Be. May The Knowledge That You Have Imbibed From This Book Lift You And Your Family To The Place Of Prominence. My God, Will Certainly imspire you to Raise A Godly Seed For You To Help Establish His Will On Earth.

THE END

DECISION PAGE

If you are not born again the promises in this book cannot be your portion because they are meant for those redeemed by the Lamb of God who takes away the sins of the world. If after reading this book you want to be born again say these words aloud wherever you are right now and Jesus will come and live in your heart.

Dear Lord Jesus forgive me for all my sins and cleanse me with your precious blood shed on the cross of Calvary. I forsake all my past evil deeds and plead that you take me and make me part of the family of God. Remove from me any curse that is following me because of my bloodline and link me to the blessings of the children of Abraham. I promise to obey and follow you all the days of my life. Please baptise me with the Holy Spirit and with power for the Christian walk.

Amen.

CONGRATULATIONS YOU ARE BORN AGAIN!!!!

If you prayed the prayer above aloud then Congratulations! You are now a born again Christian and a child of God. If you are not in any church find a well-established church which believes in the baptism of the Holy Spirit with the evidence of speaking in tongues and commit to it with all your strength, gifts and talents.

Please write to me and tell me how this book has impacted your life to the following addresses

C/O TIDD/Forestry Commission

Box 783

Takoradi

Western Region, Ghana

Email Address: lexgyi@yahoo.com or lexgyi@gmail.com

Lexgyi.blogspot.com

Instagram: lexgyi

Facebook:lexgyi@yahoo.com

Youtube: Alexander Gyimah Agyemang

Made in the USA
Middletown, DE
03 March 2024

50691306R00070